The Three Powers of Government.

The Origin of the United States; and the Status of the Southern States, on the Suppression of the Rebellion.

The Three Dangers of the Republic.

LECTURES

DELIVERED

IN THE LAW SCHOOL OF HARVARD COLLEGE, AND IN DARTMOUTH COLLEGE, 1867-68, AND '69.

BY

JOEL PARKER.

NEW YORK:
PUBLISHED BY HURD AND HOUGHTON.
Cambridge: Riverside Press.
1869.

RIVERSIDE, CAMBRIDGE:
PRINTED BY H. O. HOUGHTON AND COMPANY.

LECTURE I.

THE THREE POWERS OF GOVERNMENT.

Delivered in the Law School of Harvard College, in January, 1867, and in Dartmouth College, in April, 1869.

Gentlemen of the Law School: —

THE subject of my lecture to-day is in the department of Constitutional Law. For two years past I have devoted the closing lecture of my course for the autumn term, to some of the topics embraced in that department, which were of prominent interest in connection with passing events, and I propose to continue that arrangement.

My subject at the present time is the three great powers of government, to wit, the Legislative, Judicial, and Executive, with a view to the consideration of the appropriate functions of each, in a constitutional republic, and especially under the constitutions of the several States, and of the United States; showing the absolute necessity that they should be kept separate, and the action of each confined to its appropriate sphere.

You are at once aware, from this announcement, that I must necessarily traverse some of the debatable ground, which has recently been contested by different parties with a greater degree of zeal than of knowledge or discretion. From the prominence which has lately been given to the discussion of some portion of the subject, or, perhaps, I should rather say the prominence which has been given to violent assertions of opinion, and violent denunciations of opinion, on topics connected with the subject, it may well be supposed that you have all of you, to some extent, greater or less, formed opinions in relation to them. It is quite probable that those opinions may not be entirely alike, and perhaps the opinions which some of you have formed may be not entirely in accordance with those which I am about to express. If so, I pray you, as I have done before, to rest assured that in whatever I may say I have no party to serve, nor any party purpose to subserve, nor any personal interest to promote. Will it be too much for me to ask of your faith and trust an unhesitating confidence, that my sole purpose is to aid, as far as I may, in a sound exposition of the principles of constitutional law, particularly as they are applicable to the Constitution of the United States, which in my belief is essential to the interests of republican liberty, and to the stability of our institutions.

Government, in one sense of the term, has been defined to be "the exercise of authority; direction and restraint, exercised over the actions of men, in communities, societies, or states; the administration of public affairs, according to established constitution, laws, and usages, or by arbitrary edicts." In another sense it is "the system of polity in a state; that form of fundamental rules and principles, by which a nation or state is governed, or by which individual members of a body politic are to regulate their social actions; a constitution, either written or unwritten, by which the rights and duties of citizens and public officers are prescribed and defined."

The legitimate purpose of government in this "exercise of authority," is not merely the administration of public affairs, and the enforcement of the duties, and the imposition of the restraints which are necessary to that administration, but it is also the establishment and security of private rights, and the protection of all who are under its jurisdiction in the enjoyment of those rights, the protection of their persons from unlawful violence, of their reputation from the assaults of malice, and of their property and possessions from all unlawful interference.

Systems of government are of three sorts, Monarchical, the government of one; Oligarchical, that of a few; Democratic, that of the whole.

It is the first which is most often a despotism. But either of these three forms may be despotic. Absolute power — authority unlimited and uncontrolled, acting according to no prescribed rule, or disregarding at pleasure a rule which has been prescribed, and punishing a person for an act which was against no rule, and therefore innocent when it was done, or depriving a person of his property, according to the will of the party exercising the authority at the time — may be exercised by several persons acting as a council, or by a majority in a democracy, as well as by a single ruler whose will is the law of the state.

There are, essentially inherent, in every system of government, three principal powers, — the Legislative power, the proper office of which is to make the laws; the Judicial, which is rightly exercised in the interpretation of the laws, inquiring also into their infraction, and applying remedial justice; and the Executive, which manages the affairs of the state committed to its charge, according to the laws, and enforces, if necessary, the decrees of the judicial department.

The security of the people, in their rights of person and property, depends upon the separation of these three powers into distinct departments, and upon the adoption of rules of government which shall limit and prescribe the powers to be exercised by each department, providing that each shall operate as a check upon each of the others, in such a mode as to restrain all within their proper limits.

How to effect this is a problem not yet solved. The experience of the last few years leads to a fear that it is one which is never to be finally solved, until righteousness and peace pervade the whole earth.

In some governments the three powers are mixed and confused, without definite limits, running into each other, and perhaps retrospective and *ex post facto* in their operation, and not exercised alike in their relation to all persons and all actions.

The monarch who reigns without restraint, and whose will is the law of his realm, who directs what shall be done, and how and when it shall be done, approves or condemns at pleasure what has been done, and punishes without remorse or mercy the most venial, and even meritorious acts, with the same severity as the most atrocious crimes, is a lawgiver, a judge, and an executive potentate. It may be his pleasure to define the action which is required of his subjects, by particular rules prescribed for their observance. It may be that the rule is, that whatever is done without his permission may be treated as an offence committed. These are both instances of a rule which is prospective. It may be that he blends the legislative, judicial, and executive powers in a single action of his will, by which he regards something done, or left undone, by one of his subjects, as an offence which he punishes at his discretion. It may be that he exercises but one of these powers in a particular case. He prescribes the rule, and sees fit not to enforce it. This is legislation alone. He regards a thing which when done was not in violation of an existing rule, as a matter to be punished. This is, in its nature, an *ex post facto* law, which is promulgated, and sentence rendered, and carried into execution forthwith, by an order which forms part of the transaction, — and may be deemed to be an exercise of judicial and executive power. It may be that he regards the mere existence of one of his subjects as an obstacle to some proposed action, and by a summary order sends him to execution, in which case neither legislative nor judicial power is exercised. The act is an exercise of despotic executive power only. These instances may suffice to show us that the three powers which have been mentioned, exist, even in such a government, while it is at the pleasure of the despot which of them shall be exercised, and the manner of their exercise; the ordinary result being that the executive power is often the sole power which is brought into action.

What has thus been said of the despotic power of the monarch, is equally true of an oligarchy which may be equally a despotism.

It makes no essential difference in the principle, that the powers of government are exercised by several persons, as a supreme power. In their united action, or in the action by the voice of a majority, if that be the nature of the case, they exercise the three powers named, and may exercise them in the same manner, or omit the exercise of one or more of them at their pleasure.

It makes no difference whether this body be called a Council, a Senate, a holy Vehmé, an Inquisition, a Congress, or a *Court-martial;* or whether its acts are in the form of laws, decrees, orders, judgments, or sentences, if it exercise the supreme power of government, without restraint, at the pleasure of its will.

The same is true of a democracy, acting by majorities, and ruling without restraint. If the democracy be of limited numbers, the ruling power may resolve itself into what, if it were not the supreme power, would properly be denominated a mob; but it would not thereby have changed its character. A mob sometimes assumes to itself, and exercises all these powers. At times it makes a show of the judicial, and perhaps applies an *ex post facto* rule. But its action usually presents more of the executive feature, than of the legislative, or judicial.

I need not argue to you that there is no security for civil liberty (but that would be an inappropriate phrase), that there is no civil liberty in such a government. Property, liberty, and life itself, are held at the unchecked will of an irresponsible power. No one knows, from day to day, that he is, for an hour, secure of either. The hand of a "familiar," or an "official," or a sergeant-at-arms, or a corporal of the guard, may be laid on him at any moment; and the dungeon, the rack, the stake, the guillotine, or the gibbet, may follow, without the possibility of the intervention of any *habeas corpus*, or other stay of proceedings, except at the pleasure of the ruling power.

The sentence denounced may be unjust, without excuse or palliation. There is no power to stop it, except the power which decrees it shall be executed. The proceedings may be as secret as the grave. The husband or father, the son and brother, the wife and daughter, may disappear, without a trace left behind by which to discover the place of imprisonment or of burial; or the arrest, incarceration, and execution, may be at high noon, in the presence of weeping relatives and trembling spectators, and the doom be equally beyond any power of delay or prevention.

I have thus described some of the most odious forms of despotic power.

But there may be other forms, presenting, ostensibly, less odious characteristics, in which the powers of government may be exercised in a similar manner, but to a limited extent only, and perhaps in rare instances, and these by usurpation. Something of this kind is to be expected at the present day, rather than the absolute power of which I have just spoken. Civil liberty may exist, to some extent, greater or less. There may be, in quiet times, no cause of complaint of the administration of the government. But if the exercise of despotic rule may be admitted at all; if it is conceded that emergencies may arise when such authority may be exercised; if it is permitted to exist, even as a possibility, — to the extent of its exercise, whatever that may be, civil liberty is but at the pleasure of the government which does or may exercise it, and all persons hold their property, liberty, and lives, at the pleasure of whoever may, on one pretext or another, put in motion the engine of despotism.

One of the great struggles of the civilized world has been to shake off and overthrow despotic government, whether exhibited in one or the other of its various forms, and to substitute a government which should maintain and preserve civil liberty.

It needs no argument to show that such a government cannot be expected from an absolute monarchy, nor from any limited number of people exercising the power of government with an interest adverse to that of the whole people; nor from the great body of the people, exercising all the powers of government in mass-meeting, with no study of the principles which lie at the foundation of all good government, and subject to the influence of demagogues whose interest it is to make the worse appear the better reason.

If the people generally are ignorant, they become the prey of the designing. But education alone furnishes no guaranty for the maintenance of liberty. On the contrary, it is consistent with extraordinary corruption.

If the people are corrupt, it is in vain to expect that the government which they set up will be any better than the constituency which it represents.

In neither of these cases can it be hoped that the different powers of government will be faithfully exerted for the promotion of liberty, even if their administration is committed to separate and independent departments. But these are extreme cases.

It is in those states of society in which the great mass of the people are neither so ignorant as not to understand their rights, nor so corrupt as to barter them away, or to be regardless of them, that there is a well-founded hope for the preservation of liberty.

Even there, the best arrangements for civil government may be overturned, for the time being, by the passions of the multitude; and repentance, if it come at all, may be altogether too late to remedy the mischief which passion and recklessness have produced.

The greatest safeguard which the case admits of, — guarding against the errors of ignorance, on the one hand, and passion on the other, — guarding, so far as may be, against the corruption which sometimes contaminates numbers of the people, — is in the distribution of the powers of government into three separate departments, in the manner already indicated.

The republics of the ancient world furnished only a very limited security to civil rights.

The legislative and executive powers were generally in the hands of one person, or body of persons, and although the judicial power was nominally separated, yet, being the weaker, it could, from its nature, have but little independence when the other two were united against it. In fact it was substantially subservient, from the nature of the case.

The attempt was long since made, in England, to separate the legislative, judicial, and executive powers, and to erect them into distinct, and to some extent, independent departments of government; and by this means, and by the declaration of certain principles of right, to secure civil liberty to the people. These principles are set forth in Magna Charta, the Petition of Right, the Habeas Corpus Act, and the Bill of Rights.

Mr. John Adams in the preface to the "Defence of the American Constitutions," published in London, in 1787, says: "The people's rights and liberties, and the democratical mixture in a constitution, can never be preserved without a strong executive, or, in other words, without separating the executive power from the legislative. If the executive power, or any considerable part of it, is left in the hands either of an aristocratical or a democratical assembly, it will corrupt the legislature, as necessarily as rust corrupts iron, or as arsenic poisons the human body; and when the legislature is corrupted, the people are undone."

After quoting Tacitus, as doubting the practicability, or the duration, of a republic in which there is a governor, or senate, and a house of representatives, though he admits the theory to be laudable; and Cicero, as declaring the superiority of such a government, Mr. Adams says: "As all the ages of the world have not produced a greater statesman and philosopher, united in the same character, his authority should have great weight. His decided opinion, in favor of three branches, is founded on a reason that is unchangeable; the laws, which are the only possible rule, measure, and security of justice, can be sure of protection, for any course of time, in no other form of government."

He then says: "If Cicero and Tacitus could revisit the

earth, and learn that the English nation had reduced the great idea to practice, and brought it nearly to perfection, by giving each division a power to defend itself by a negative; had found it the most solid and durable government, as well as the most free; had obtained, by means of it, a prosperity among civilized nations, in an enlightened age, like that of the Romans among barbarians; and that the Americans, after having enjoyed the benefit of such a constitution a century and a half, were advised by some of the greatest philosophers and politicians of the age to renounce it, and set up the governments of ancient Goths and modern Indians, — what would they say? That the Americans would be more reprehensible than the Cappadocians, if they should listen to such advice."

But the negative in the monarch of the English Constitution is merely nominal, being never exercised; and it is for this reason, and from the fact that there is in the English unwritten constitution no recognized power otherwise limiting the legislative authority of Parliament, that that body is often termed omnipotent. If Parliament refuses to sanction the measures of the ministry, who represent the king, the ministry resign, or the king dissolves Parliament, and there is a new election. If measures are adopted by Parliament against the will of the existing administration, the ministry resign or acquiesce. But there is no power, on the part of the judicial department, to declare any act of Parliament void, because in violation of Magna Charta, or against the Petition of Right, for even these are not recognized as the supreme law of the land, unalterable except by the act of the great body of the people; the first being a grant or declaration by the king, and the latter a parliamentary declaration of right.

Montesquieu, in his chapter on the Constitution of England, says: —

"When the legislative and executive powers are united in the same person, or in the same body of magistrates, there can be no liberty; because apprehensions may arise, lest the same monarch or senate should enact tyrannical laws, to execute them in a tyrannical manner."

Again: —

"There is no liberty if the power of judging be not separated from the legislative and executive powers. Were it joined with the legislative, the life and liberty of the subject would be exposed to arbitrary control; for the judge would then be the legislator. Were it joined to the executive power, the judge might behave with all the violence of an oppressor.

"There would be an end of everything like liberty were the same man, or the same body, whether of the nobles or of the people, to exercise those three powers: that of enacting laws, that of executing the public resolutions, and that of judging the crimes or differences of individuals.

"Most kingdoms in Europe enjoy a moderate government, because the prince, who is invested with the two first powers, leaves the third to his subjects. In Turkey, where these three powers are united in the Sultan's person, the subjects groan under the weight of a most frightful oppression.

"In the republics of Italy, where these three powers are united, there is less liberty than in our monarchies. Hence their government is obliged to have recourse to as violent methods for its support, as even that of the Turks; witness the state inquisitors, and the lion's mouth into which every informer may at all hours throw his written accusations.

"What a situation must the poor subject be in, under those republics! The same body of magistrates are possessed, as executors of the laws, of the whole power they have given themselves in quality of legislators. They may plunder the state by their general determinations; and as they have likewise the judiciary in their hands, every private citizen may be ruined by their particular decisions.

"The whole power is here united in one body; and though there is no external pomp that indicates a despotic sway, yet the people feel the effects of it every moment."

There are under the English Constitution checks which in some measure compensate for the lack of a negative by one department of the government upon the proceedings of the other.

The monarch is nominally possessed of the executive power, but he is surrounded by a ministry who mainly exercise it in fact, and who are held responsible for its exercise. The monarch is irresponsible, — can do no wrong politically. But if the ministry transcend the existing laws they are held accountable, criminally and civilly, unless they can obtain an act of indemnity. The power of the king to dissolve the Parliament is a prerogative check upon a parliamentary encroachment. The legislative power is deposited in two branches, the members of one branch holding their seats generally by hereditary right, those of the other through elections by the people ; the interests of the two classes not being identical, sometimes even antagonistic, and the hereditary branch opposing a conservative check upon radical changes which may be desired by the other. At the same time the executive, by a power to create peers, who thereby become members of that branch, holds a check upon it, which may prevent its conservatism from interposing an obstacle to reform, or its hereditary aristocracy from becoming dangerous to the crown. Parliament, on the other hand, has the power to refuse supplies, and thus paralyze the action of the executive, and check obnoxious measures. And the judiciary, although the incumbents of the bench are appointed by the crown, are, from the tenure of their appointment, as independent, as the nature of the case will admit, of both king and Parliament.

The three powers of government being thus placed in separate departments, it remains to be seen whether these checks do not practically provide for the security of liberty, at least equally well with a form which is, theoretically, more perfect, by means of negatives which the different departments have on each other. They will provide as effectually for that security, if these negatives shall practically lose their theoretical force and themselves become nugatory.

One of the great objects of a considerable portion of the early settlers of this country was to obtain the security of civil rights as well as of religious liberty. But it was not to be expected that in the infancy of the colonies, dependent as they were to a great extent upon the crown, and separated into distinct communities, any well-defined arrangement of the powers of government could be perfected by them. It was only after the declaration of independence that the people had an opportunity to devise and adopt a more perfect system than that of Great Britain (theoretically at least), for the security of civil liberty, by the formation of written constitutions, which *in theory* are the fundamental law prescribed by the people, as the source of political power. These not only separated the three great powers of government, and placed them in separate departments, but limited and controlled the action of the departments by the declaration of fundamental principles, which none of the departments, nor even all of them combined, might lawfully disregard or violate. And further, by the adoption of checks, conferring, to an extent, greater or less, the power of restraint in each upon the action of the other, in the exercise of the powers granted, civil liberty and civil rights were to be guarded by the independent action of each in its separate sphere.

Upon the declaration of independence the people of the new States proceeded to organize State governments, each State for itself. Some of them continued to act under their original charters, as the foundation of their government, but most of them framed written constitutions, which became the organic law of their respective States. Even before the final adoption of the Declaration of Independence by Congress, Virginia formed such a constitution, consisting of a Bill of Rights and a Form of Government.[1] Other States followed. Some with separate bills of rights, and others incorporating assertions of right and principle into the frame-work of their form of government. At a later period a Constitution was adopted by the peoples of all the States for the limited purposes expressed in it, which contained an express provision that "this constitution, and the laws of the United States which shall be made in pursuance thereof, and all treaties made or which shall be made, under the authority of the United States, shall be the supreme law of the land; and the judges in every State shall be bound thereby, anything in the constitution or laws of any State to the contrary notwithstanding."

The principles of the State constitutions for the security of civil liberty were afterwards expressly incorporated into it, in the shape of amendments.

[1] It has been denied that the States were at any time sovereign. That position cannot be maintained. Without entering into the argument here, it may be well to say, in this connection, that in this adoption of a Constitution, — a fundamental law for the foundation of civil government within her borders, defining the rights and liabilities of her citizens, — a law which had no rule or authority above it, and which was therefore the exercise of the highest possible attribute of sovereignty, — Virginia neither asked the permission of Congress, nor submitted her constitution to the revision of that body. And although Massachusetts and some other of the colonies asked the advice of Congress in relation to "taking up civil government," no one of the States ever asked permission to adopt a constitution, or submitted that which the people had adopted, or proposed to adopt, to Congress for the sanction or approbation of that body. There was no power in Congress to control the action of the States in the adoption of their fundamental law, and of course none in regard to any other law.

In these constitutional provisions of the States, and of the United States, — in the separation of the legislative, executive, and judicial powers, — in the independence of each, within its proper sphere, — and in the checks which are provided, to prevent, as far as may be possible, encroachments by either, — rests the great security of civil liberty in this country.

It was reserved to the judicial department of the United States to declare, that by the written fundamental law thus prescribed in the Constitution of the United States, there existed a power in that department to guard against any infringement of such rights of the people as were protected in that supreme law and might be within the jurisdiction of that department, by a judicial decision declaring the absolute nullity of any act of the legislative department, which should be passed in violation of the provisions of the Constitution.

This, however, was but a legitimate result from the fact that the people had prescribed a paramount law, binding upon all officers of the government, as well as upon the people; and the fact that the judicial department is, in all cases which its process can reach, the interpreter and judge of the law of the land.

The same principle is applicable to the constitutions of the several States, so far as they are not controlled by the Constitution of the United States.

Our constitutions doubtless admit of improvement in some of their details. But these improvements are not to be looked for at the hands of those who make flaming speeches about the march of knowledge, and who decry the labors of the original framers of the fundamental laws of the States and of the nation.

The original constitutions were framed in times which brought the great principles of civil liberty, and the true rights and interests of the people, prominently into view, and when parties had not been formed to serve the ambitious projects of those who were seeking to acquire, or preserve, power and place. They were formed by men better versed in the history of the ancient republics than those who are now crying out for change. They were formed in times favorable for a calm and temperate consideration of the momentous questions involved in the formation of a fundamental paramount law. And it will be the part of wisdom in their successors, to consider and deliberate, as carefully and intelligently as they did, before any action is taken which shall ignore or violate the fundamental principles upon which they based their action.

If they considered slavery a subject respecting which it was expedient to make compromises for the sake of union, it was certainly not the part of wisdom in their successors, in the slave States, to cherish and extend that institution, instead of providing for a gradual emancipation. And it remains to be seen how far it was and is wise, in the successors of those persons in the free States who deemed it better to secure a united government over the whole country than to go to war upon objections to that institution, — to break the bonds of the slave suddenly, and entirely, and then to endanger all the principles of civil liberty, by a controversy whether the newly emancipated slave shall at once have the right of suffrage. The emancipation has imposed hardship, misery, disease, and death upon immense numbers of those whom it set free. If it shall be the means of breaking down the divisions which separate the legislative, executive, and judicial powers, and thus of destroying the safeguards of civil liberty, our successors may yet have bitter occasion to believe, that bad as African slavery must be acknowledged to be, the loss of all security for persons and property is an evil of infinitely greater magnitude.

The safeguards of civil liberty provided by the wisdom of the fathers have certainly been sadly prostrated in the time of the children, and the end is not yet. At the very first strain upon them they gave way, partly on the plea of necessity, — the tyrant's plea, — which often means mere questionable expediency, — partly by reason of the personal ambition which leads the individual to seek his own elevation without regard to the rights of others, and which induces him to excite and mislead the people, in order to promote and secure his own selfish ends, — an ambition which has been in all ages the curse of political rights and civil freedom.

The first breach in the defences of constitutional liberty, during the late war, was in the adoption of new and extreme constructions of the Constitution of the United States, particularly in that construction of the "war power" which caused it to overshadow all the other powers of the government, and made the President a despotic ruler. He could do whatever the necessity of the hour required, he being at the same time, the sole judge when the necessity existed, and what it required.

Strange as may now seem this assertion of the despotic power of the Executive, it found ready adherents, and became, with the party in power, almost a recognized axiom in the interpretation of the Constitution, even among those who are now quite as ready to maintain an equally engrossing and despotic power in Congress. With them the war is not yet ended, and it will not be until their selfish ends and purposes are accomplished and secured.

I propose to call your attention to some of the evidences of this assumption of power by the Executive, and by Congress.

Of that great humbug, the emancipation proclamation, which Mr. Lincoln at the time compared to the Pope's bull against the comet, — and of which Mr. Thaddeus Stevens of Pennsylvania said, recently, that "no thoughtful man ever supposed that it liberated a single slave," I have spoken and written heretofore. "Noble in sentiment," he said ; but it must stand as one of the evidences of the readiness of the persons then in power to disregard the provisions of the Constitution, respecting the rights of the States and of the people.

It has been asserted that if it did not liberate the slaves, it had a great effect in securing the success of the war. On the contrary, in my opinion, it had a direct tendency at the time to jeopardize its success. It doubtless gratified radical politicians, who should have given their hearty support to the prosecution of the war without it; but it cooled the zeal of others, who, however earnestly they might have desired the emancipation of the slaves, by any constitutional means, yet saw in it the inauguration of a system of measures, under a pretext of the "war power," which could have no legitimate existence under the Constitution, and which, while professing to make freemen of slaves, in fact made slaves of freemen. Certainly its direct tendency was to induce the rebels to fight with greater desperation.[1]

[1] The effect of the proclamation, in exciting enthusiasm in support of the war, if to be found anywhere, must have exhibited itself in Massachusetts. The fact, however, that not even a company of volunteers was raised in Massachusetts after the proclamation was issued; but that the quota of troops required from that State, subsequently, was made up by the hardest of drafting, and by sending to Canada and Germany for white men, and all over the country for negroes, shows that the proclamation, if it had any effect, operated as a wet blanket.

The attempt, by a presidential proclamation, to declare martial law over the whole of the United States, and to suspend the habeas corpus throughout the length and breadth of the land, without regard to the existence of active military hostilities in particular localities, was an act of a kindred character, so far as constitutional power was involved, but much more mischievous in its pretensions.

A departure from its proper province has not been confined to the Executive department. With less of excuse, if possible, Congress has quite as signally violated the principles which should limit the action of that department; first, by attempting to confer unconstitutional power upon the President; afterwards by endeavoring to concentrate power in itself.

The Constitution provides that the privilege of the writ of habeas corpus shall not be suspended unless when in cases of rebellion or invasion the public safety may require it.

I have heretofore had occasion to maintain that this is a restriction and limitation of the power of suspension, and not a grant of such a power.

It is true that the government of the United States is a limited government, having only the powers expressly granted, or such as are incident to those powers, and it is true also that there is no grant of a power, in terms, to issue the writ of habeas corpus, or of a right to suspend it.

But the right to constitute courts carried with it, as an incident, the right to regulate the process and proceedings of those courts, within the limits of the jurisdiction authorized by the Constitution ; and among other things to authorize the issue of the writ of habeas corpus, as well as other writs ; and of course to prescribe, by law, the times and seasons, terms and conditions, in and upon which it should be granted or refused.

Under this general incidental authority, the right to regulate the writ is clearly a legislative power, in regard to the suspension of the privilege of the writ, as well as in regard to the issuing of it.

The framers of the Constitution, well aware that an unlimited power to suspend the privilege of this great safeguard of civil liberty would be liable to great abuse, inserted this clause of restriction and limitation upon the power of Congress in this respect.

The connection of the clause in the Constitution serves to show, that even if it were to be regarded as a grant of a power of suspension, the power is a legislative and not an executive power. And this has been its practical construction, for the original proclamation of Mr. Lincoln suspending the privilege of the writ, was not deemed, even by his political friends, a rightful exercise of executive power under the Constitution, as is fully shown by the fact that Congress passed an act, purporting to authorize the President to suspend it, when in his judgment the public safety should require it.

But this power of suspension, being a legislative power, it is not competent for Congress to grant away, or transfer it, any more than it is competent for that body to give to the President the power to say when and on what terms and conditions it shall be issued in the first instance. This is clear, upon the general principle that no legislative body can transfer and assign any of its powers of legislation. But the conclusion that the power to suspend cannot be assigned, or committed to the Executive, is apparent, further, from the fact that this clause of limitation shows that a judgment is to be exercised as to the time when the privilege may be suspended, within, and according to the limits of the Constitution. "The privilege" . . . . "shall not be suspended, unless when in cases of rebellion or invasion the public safety may require it."

The question whether there is rebellion or invasion is to be determined by the proper authority, in reference to this subject. But it is not sufficient to authorize the suspension, that there is rebellion or invasion, — for that alone may not show that the public safety requires the suspension. There must be a judgment exercised at the time, not only that there is rebellion or invasion, but that the public safety does or may require the suspension ; and this right of judgment involves the exercise of discretion on the part of the party who possesses, and may exercise the authority. It is perfectly clear that Congress possesses the power to exercise this judgment and discretion, and it follows with equal clearness, that it is its *duty* to judge ; and that the *power* and *duty* cannot be assigned to another department, either executive or judicial.

Another violation of constitutional duty by the two Houses of Congress of a different character, and perhaps one which the

Supreme Court cannot reach, is found in a surrender by each to the other, of a part of its constitutional power, by a joint resolution, in these words: —

"Be it resolved by the House of Representatives (the Senate concurring), That in order to close agitation upon a question which seems likely to disturb the action of the government, as well as to quiet the uncertainty which is agitating the minds of the people of the eleven States which have been declared to be in insurrection, no senator or representative shall be admitted into either branch of Congress, from any of said States, until Congress shall have declared such States entitled to representation."

If this was to be regarded as an act of legislation, so that the resolution is to have force as a law, it would be void; because the two Houses have assumed to act without the approval of the President. It would be a usurpation, the Constitution requiring that every order, resolution, or vote, to which the concurrence of the Senate and House of Representatives may be necessary, except on a question of adjournment, shall be presented to the President, who may interpose his objections.

But a distinction seems to be made between a *joint* resolution and a *concurrent* resolution, and no doubt this resolution was *a little private arrangement between the two Houses, — a bargain respecting the exercise of the power severally possessed by each of judging of the election of its own members.* Such is its true character, and as such, if it had taken the shape and form of ordinary legislation, with the prefix, "Be it enacted," or "Be it resolved, by the Senate and House of Representatives," and if it had been presented to and approved by the President, that would not have rendered it a constitutional act. I admit, that with the President's approval, it would have been no better than it is at present.

The Constitution provides that each House shall be the "judge of the elections, returns, and qualifications of its own members." There is a *duty*, as well as a *power*, of judgment.

From the very terms of the provision, the power granted is a several power; and thus it involves a several duty. It is not the subject-matter for a bargain between them. Neither House can confer upon the other any power to judge in relation to the subject, or agree to act in the matter according to the judgment of the other; and so they cannot agree that they will jointly judge of the elections and qualifications of the members of both Houses. That would clearly be in violation of the provision that each shall judge of its own.

If, then, they cannot agree to judge jointly, they cannot agree that the one shall not judge and act without the consent of the other, or until a certain contingency shall happen, for that is an attempt to limit the action of each as to time, which is as much matter for the judgment of each, as any other part of the duty relating to the subject.

If we were to suppose this resolution to be valid, the result would be, that the House has tied its hands by a bargain, so that it cannot perform its constitutional duty without the consent of the Senate; and that the Senate cannot perform its constitutional duty without the consent of the House; and this in relation to a matter respecting which the Constitution has explicitly provided that each has a separate duty to perform.

It was said by a senator who supported the resolution, "It is a mere legislative declaration of our opinion and determination, that until Congress has declared the State (whichever one it may be that is before us) to be in a condition to be represented here, neither body will act upon the credentials of members. This admits that the action is legislative in its character, and this legislative declaration of their opinion and determination, is neither more nor less than a legislative bargain.

The House initiate it, "Resolved (the Senate concurring)," and the Senate concur, that is they agree. It was made a "concurrent resolution," because it was intended merely that the two Houses should agree, and not that the President should be asked to approve.

The same senator said: "Even after we have done it, after we have made that legislative declaration," . . . . "we as a Senate, I concede, can, in spite of this legislative declaration, at any moment take them" (the credentials) "from the table and act upon them, without asking the consent of the House of Representatives; and the House can, on its own side, in spite of this resolution, if passed, take the credentials of those claiming to be members of that House, and act upon them if it pleases."

But a "*legislative declaration*" by both Houses, concurring in a resolution, is an act of legislation, and this act of concurrent legislation provides that no senator or representative shall be admitted, &c. It is not a declaration of each House of its intention to govern its own action in a particular mode.

If this agreement of the two Houses is not binding on them, as it is thus admitted that it is not, it is precisely because it is unconstitutional for them thus to agree, by reason of the constitutional provision that each shall be the judge of its own elections. It is not the less a bargain, because it is not binding. It has not been the less abided by and acted on as a bargain, because it is thus unconstitutional. That is the very objection to it. If it had been a valid agreement the objection would fail.

This denial of the right of representation until Congress shall have declared such States entitled to representation seems to be placed upon two grounds: one, that it is the constitutional right of the two Houses of Congress to judge of the election of their own members, which is violated by the very resolution itself; the other, that an inquiry is to be made whether the States whose right of representation is in question are in the union. Sometimes the two are connected in a single proposition in this form, — The two Houses are empowered to judge of the election of their own members, and must therefore inquire whether the States, from which persons present themselves as members, are in the Union or not.

That such an inquiry may be made, in the case of an attempt to send senators and representatives by a community or territorial organization never yet in the Union, is true. But it is not true in relation to States already admitted. Until a revolution takes place, an inquiry whether they are in the Union for the purpose of representation, is preposterous. They cannot rightfully be denied representation on any plea that they are not in the Union, because they cannot take themselves out of the Union, nor be turned out of the Union, except by revolution.

But this bargain, by which the two Houses undertake to limit their constitutional powers, and to surrender their constitutional duties, is only part and parcel of a more stupendous departure from the limits of their constitutional authority, by a denial that the States in question have a right to be represented in their respective Houses.

The purpose of this denial, it is admitted, is to compel the States to adopt certain proposed constitutional amendments, and perhaps to amend their own constitutions, also, beyond the terms and scope of the amendments so proposed. It does not appear how much, or what, is to be required, before the two Houses,. acting under their bargain, will consent to exercise their duty of judgment. The adoption of amendments proposed will probably be deemed enough, provided it shall clearly appear that the adoption will secure the dominant party in the possession of the offices. If there is a well founded doubt of that, then more must be required. This is the most charitable supposition, for if this is not the object, it must be revenge and vengeance, passions which it must not be surmised are the motives of legislation.

Its pretext is that the States which are thus denied a representation have revolted and thereby lost their right of representation, and cannot be entitled to it again until they are reconstructed, and that this reconstruction is within the power and a part of the duty of Congress.

If those States have lost their rights, and are not in the Union, then the Union is dissolved, so far as they are concerned. On what ground are we to arrive at such a conclusion? If we reach that conclusion, or a conclusion, on any ground, that they are not in the Union, how are they to adopt a constitutional amendment?

The passage of acts for the confiscation of property, as a punishment for offences committed against the United States, the confiscation to be made effectual without trial and conviction of the alleged offence, is another departure from the duty and power of the legislative department. It is an attempt to assume, or to transfer to military tribunals, the functions belonging to the judicial department, — is of a most dangerous character, and against an express provision of the Constitution that "the trial of all crimes, except in cases of impeachment, shall be by jury."

On the 9th of April, 1866, Congress passed, over the veto of the President, "an act to protect all persons in the United States in their civil rights and furnish the means of their vindication."

The first section of it is in these words, "That all persons born in the United States, and not subject to any foreign power, excluding Indians, not taxed, are hereby declared to be citizens of the United States; and such citizens of every race and color, without regard to any previous condition of slavery or involuntary servitude, except as a punishment for crime whereof the party shall have been duly convicted, shall have the same right in every State and Territory in the United States to make and enforce contracts; to sue, be parties, and give evidence; to inherit, purchase, lease, sell, hold, and convey real and personal property; and to full and equal benefit of all laws and proceedings for the security of person and property, as is enjoyed by white citizens, and shall be subject to like punishment, pains, and penalties, and to none other, any law, statute, ordinance, regulation, or custom, to the contrary notwithstanding."

I reserve for another occasion an inquiry into the right of Congress to create citizens otherwise than by naturalization laws, and the acquisition of territory.

The other sections provide for an enforcement of the act by very extraordinary provisions for that purpose. No judge can make a decision against its constitutionality, without incurring a heavy penalty if his decision should be reversed, and certainly no judge can have any policy of insurance or guaranty against such reversal, in the existing state of things, however clear his legal convictions may be on the subject. The only course, therefore, for any judge of inferior jurisdiction, in order to make sure of avoiding fine and imprisonment, is to decide that the law is constitutional, notwithstanding he may be convinced beyond all possible doubt of its unconstitutionality, and he is under oath to perform his official duties faithfully.

That the judicial function of impartial unbiased judgment is uprooted by such legislation needs no argument. It is in this particular a most gross interference with the appropriate duty of the judicial department. If it was not expressly intended to terrify the incumbents of the bench, its framers were unfortunate in its construction.

I omit at this time specification of other constitutional objections, as the discussion would require more time than can be spared upon the present occasion. Suffice it to say that it is, in the length and breadth of it, a gross usurpation.

With such asssumptions of power, and such violations of constitutional duty, by the Executive and Congress, we might surely infer that the exercise of arbitrary power would be common in the War and Navy Departments.

Two or three instances may serve as examples of what may be expected from the "war power," when it overrides constitutional safeguards.

General Charles P. Stone was arrested under pretence of responsibility for the disaster of Ball's Bluff, and on vague accusations of other offences. He was in the military service, and therefore legitimately amenable to a court-martial, having a right to have charges and specifications filed against him, and to a trial.

But this was no part of the purpose of his accusers. He had been a right arm to General Scott, in providing for the protection of Washington, at a time when its possession by the rebels would have secured their independence. No one really doubted that he was a skillful, brave, and gallant officer. The primary cause of his arrest was probably to draw off the attention of the people from the failure of a favorite political partisan, then recently appointed a major-general, and who commanded at Ball's Bluff. I have been so assured by a gentleman who held a high command in that battle.

But it was understood, further, that General Stone had said something of a senator which was not entirely respectful, and that he was not a person who could be brought to coöperate in the favorite measures of the party. And so he was imprisoned a long time in Fort Lafayette, his repeated demands for charges and a trial disregarded, and his prospects of success in his chosen profession ruined, at the will of the Secretary of War, in violation not only of the Constitution, but of express provisions of legislation for the government of the army.

The proceedings had no warrant of law, military or civil. It was a most oppressive use of despotic power, assumed by usurpation, to serve partisan purposes, and one for which no atonement has ever been made.

Smith, Brothers & Co., of Boston, were contractors for supplies for the use of the Navy Department, and fell under the displeasure of Lieut. Wise and some of his associates in the Navy Department.

Their real offence seems to have been that they refused to become participators in frauds upon the government. In 1864, a charge was made against them that they themselves had defrauded it. They were arrested by military authority, imprisoned in Fort Warren, and bail in half a million of dollars required. When they had prepared to give security in this enormous amount, the demand was abated to $20,000 each. Their houses were entered, and their repositories searched; their store broken open, the lock of the safe forced, and their books and papers carried away; and a court-martial was ordered for their trial *in Philadelphia.*

Fortunately for them they had made their mark as adherents of the republican party and were thereby enabled to enlist senatorial and other influences in their favor. This reduced the bail, and obtained an order that the trial (which it was intended should be far away from their witnesses and means of defence) should be at Boston, where the offence, if any, had been committed; giving them, by a presidential countermand, what they should have had at first as a common right.

The principal witness had previously written to his confidant, "I have been summoned before the select committee of the Senate for investigating frauds in naval supplies, and if the wool don't fly it won't be my fault. Norton, the Navy agent, has complained that I have interfered with his business. He and his friend Smith are dead cocks in the pit. We have got a sure thing on them, in the tin business. They that dance must pay the fiddler." — So far as he was able, he secured the success of his prediction that the wool would fly. "When a case comes to my oath, it 's a won cause," said poor Peter Peebles, and so thought the naval officer.

The trial was of great length, involving serious charges of fraud, and the examination of extended accounts amounting to a million and a quarter of dollars. But the charges were all triumphantly met and refuted. They were abandoned, substantially, by the prosecution, except the single one of substituting Revely for Banca tin, and thereby, as was contended, defrauding the government of $100.

The fact that Revely tin was furnished, instead of Banca, was not denied; but the charge of fraud was negatived by ample evidence to show that this was because Banca tin could not be procured just at the time when the tin was to be delivered; that Revely tin was just as good for the purpose for which it was wanted, as the other; and by the testimony of the master founder at the yard where it was to be used, that for seven years they had used no other than Revely. The testimony of merchants, chemists, and assayers, was also introduced to show that there was in fact no difference between the two. But all this was insufficient. "Fie on your civil courts," was the language of a high officer in the Navy Department; "your civil courts are organized to acquit. We organize courts to convict." And so it proved.

This contempt of civil courts, and avowed purpose of military tribunals, shows the total insecurity of civil rights in a government ruling by military commissions and courts-martial. Convictions are "a sure thing." The court-martial that tried Messrs. Smith, found them guilty of the tin; and sentenced them to pay a fine of $20,000, and to be imprisoned for two years.

The revising counsel for the Navy Department attempted to sustain the decision; but the senatorial influence was again brought to bear in favor of the faithful. The President committed the case to the senator for a report, who justly, and properly, exonerated Messrs. Smith from all blame, and the President disapproved of the proceedings, annulled the judgment and sentence, and ordered the accused to be discharged, perhaps in terms not very complimentary to the court, or others who were active in promoting the prosecution, as Messrs. Smith have not been able to obtain from the Navy Department a copy of his order.

It can "need no ghost come from the grave to tell us," that if Messrs. Smith had been among those who believed that the government did sometimes lay its hand wrongfully upon some of the people, they would have had a further and most woeful experience of the insecurity of civil liberty when the sovereign powers are exercised by a single department, without checks or restraints. One of those gentlemen had, recently before his arrest, expressed the opinion, that the government did not put its hand upon any one without good reason. His adherence to the party stood him in good stead, in procuring the reversal of the sentence, although even that could not withstand the malice of the prosecution, and the subservience of the court. And it is quite probable that his faith in relation to unwarrantable arrests has been somewhat shaken by his experience in this matter.

Lambdin P. Milligan was a citizen of Indiana, where he had resided twenty years, and had never been in the military or naval service of the United States. On the 5th of October, 1864, while at his home, he was arrested by the order of the general commanding the military district of Indiana, and from that period was for a long time kept in close confinement. On the 21st of October, 1864, he was tried by a military commission, convened by order of the general, on certain charges and specifications (substantially, it seems, that he belonged to a secret organization, which was conspiring to assist the enemy), was found guilty, and sentenced to be hanged. An order from the War Department stated that the sentence had been approved by the President, and directed that it be carried into execution immediately. An order was issued that he should be hung on the 19th of July, 1865. On the 10th of that month, Milligan presented a petition to the Circuit Court of the United States for a habeas corpus, and a discharge from his imprisonment. The petition stated that since his arrest, the Circuit Court had held a session, empanelled and discharged a grand jury, and that no bill of indictment had been found against him ; and he claimed that he should be turned over to the proper civil tribunal, to be proceeded against according to the law of the land, or discharged from custody under the provision of the act of Congress of March 5th, 1863 ; insisting that the military commission had no right to try him upon any charges whatever, because he was a citizen of the United States, and of the State of Indiana, and had not been, since the commencement of the rebellion, in any of the States whose citizens were arrayed against the government of the United States, and that the right of trial by jury was guarantied to him by the Constitution of the United States.

The judges of the Circuit Court were divided in opinion upon the subject, and the division was certified to the Supreme Court of the United States. In this tribunal all the judges agreed that Milligan was entitled to be discharged. But they divided, five to four, upon some of the principles which were involved in the determination of the case.

I have thus referred to a very few of the many instances furnished by the late war, of the insecurity of life, and of civil rights, under a system, which, on whatever pretext, places despotic power in a single individual department.

I have not adverted to the trial of the conspirators for the assassination of President Lincoln and Secretary Seward, because I am disposed to regard that as an exceptional case in relation to some of the accused.

There was hardly a decent pretence for regarding the offence as one which could be brought under the cognizance of a military tribunal. There was just about as much of a legal pretext for that, as there was for the refusal of Mr. Secretary Stanton to permit Mr. Ford, the owner, to sell the theatre in which Mr. Lincoln was assassinated.

But after much thought, and some misgiving, I am inclined to acquiesce in the administration of lynch law upon very extraordinary occasions, and in very extreme cases, and to regard this case as one of that character. It had the form of a trial by a military commission, appointed for the purpose, but that was little better than a solemn farce. The Western "Regulators" sometimes go through the form of a trial by jury, and hang the subjects of their assumed jurisdiction, only after the rendition of a verdict, being predetermined from the outset to hang them; and so in this case. The execution of Mrs. Surratt was no better than any other murder.

While the executive power, which but a few years since was exalted by party politicians above the judicial, and even above the legislative also, has recently been swallowed up by the legislative branch, to a very great extent, the judicial department is exhibiting a partial independence, manifested, however, in some measure by a mere major vote.

In the case of Milligan, to which reference has already been made, the majority of the court sustained these propositions: —

"Military commissions, organized during the late civil war, in a State not invaded and not engaged in rebellion, in which the Federal courts were open, and in the proper and unobstructed exercise of their judicial functions, had no jurisdiction to try, convict, or sentence for any criminal offence, a citizen who was neither a resident of a rebellious State, nor a prisoner of war, nor a person in the naval or military service. And Congress could not invest them with any such power."

"The guaranty of trial by jury contained in the Constitution was intended for a state of war, as well as a state of peace; and is equally binding upon rulers and people, at all times and under all circumstances."

"The Federal authority having been unopposed in the State of Indiana, and the Federal courts open for the trial of offences and the redress of grievances, the usages of war could not, under the Constitution, afford any sanction for the trial there of a citizen in civil life, not connected with the military or naval service, by a military tribunal, for any offence whatever."

So far very well. But a minority of four judges, speaking through the Chief Justice, take occasion to sustain that construction of the Constitution which subjects all civil liberty to military power in time of war.

There are two or three matters in this opinion of the four judges which deserve your careful consideration. It is said: —

"The power to make the necessary laws is in Congress; the power to execute in the President. Both powers imply many subordinate and auxiliary powers. Each includes all authorities essential to its due exercise. But neither can the President in war more than in peace, intrude upon the proper authority of Congress, nor Congress upon the proper authority of the President. Both are servants of the people, whose will is expressed in the fundamental law. Congress cannot direct the conduct of campaigns, nor can the President, or any commander under him, without the sanction of Congress, institute tribunals for the trial and punishment of offences, either of soldiers or civilians, *unless in cases of a controlling necessity, which justifies what it compels, or at least insures acts of indemnity from the justice of the legislature.*

"We by no means assert that Congress can establish and apply the laws of war where no war has been declared or exists."

"Where peace exists, the laws of peace must prevail. What we do maintain is, that when the nation is involved in war, and some portions of the country are invaded, and all are exposed to invasion, *it is within the power of Congress to determine in what States or Districts such great and imminent public danger exists as justifies the authorization of military tribunals for the trial of crimes and offences against the discipline or security of the army, or against the public safety.*"

"We have confined ourselves to the question of power. It was for Congress to determine the question of expediency. And Congress did determine it. That body did not see fit to authorize trials by military commission in Indiana, but by the strongest implication prohibited them. With that prohibition we are satisfied, and should have remained silent if the answers to the questions certified had been put on that ground, without denial of the existence of a power which we believe to be constitutional and important to the public safety; *a denial of which, as we have already suggested, seems to draw in question the power of Congress to protect from prosecution the members of military commissions, who acted in obedience to their superior officers, and whose action, whether warranted by law or not, was approved by that upright and patriotic President, under whose administration the republic was rescued from threatened destruction.*"

I shall not detain you at this time with an argument to show that this places the liberties of the whole country, and all its inhabitants, in the power of Congress, in time of war, if it pleases Congress to assume that there is great public danger. The safeguards of the Constitution of the United States, and those of the constitutions and laws of the several States, are swept away also in cases of "controlling necessity," of which the President may judge, — a necessity which justifies what it is supposed to compel, or at least insures acts of indemnity from the justice of the legislature. — A necessity to do what the Constitution and laws will punish as a wrongful act, is not a necessity which the Constitution can recognize.

And what is this indemnity thus spoken of? Not merely a provision of a pecuniary character, to reimburse the expense and loss to which those who execute the unlawful measures of the President and of Congress may be subjected, by actions to recover damages in the courts of justice. We are further enlightened on that subject, by a subsequent paragraph in the same opinion. It is a power, by means of subsequent legislation, to protect from prosecution members of military commissions, who act in obedience to their superior officers, whether that action is warranted by law or not, provided it was approved by President Lincoln. We are not informed whether the approval of any other patriotic President, who may sit in the executive chair during another war, will authorize Congress to pass subsequent acts of protection for unlawful acts.

It may well be maintained, that the legislature may provide, by a prospective law, for the protection of an executive officer, who is required by his superior to serve process, and who is unable to judge whether the command is lawful or not; but the power asserted here by the minority of the court, for Congress, is, not only to make the party who exercises an assumed right of judgment, and issues his commands for death, imprisonment, or fine, in a case where he had no right whatever to sit in judgment, irresponsible for his acts, however atrocious they may be; but to do this by a statute passed after the fact, and thus, in cases of trespass and imprisonment, to take away a vested right of action existing at the time.

This is done by the omnipotent Parliament of Great Britain; but what clause of the Constitution of the United States confers such a power upon Congress, the minority of the Supreme Court do not inform us.

Since the foregoing remarks were written a bill of indemnity has been introduced into the House by the Judiciary Committee.[1]

This, however, is not the sole instance in which the minority of the court attempt to maintain a right of Congress to pass retrospective laws, depriving a party of vested rights, although

[1] The bill exhibits very clearly the extent of the power claimed. If such a power may be exercised in this class of cases, what shall prevent its exercise in every other case, at the pleasure of Congress.

"*Be it enacted, &c.*, That all acts, proclamations, and orders of the President of the United States, or acts done by his authority or approval, after the 4th of March, 1861, and before the 1st of December, 1865, respecting martial law, military trials by court-martial or military commissions, or the arrest, imprisonment, and trial of persons charged with participation in the late rebellion against the United States, or as aiders or abettors thereof, or as guilty of any disloyal practice in aid thereof, or of any violation of the laws or usages of war, or of affording aid and comfort to rebels against the authority of the United States; and all proceedings and acts done or had by courts-martial or military commissions, or arrests and imprisonments made in the premises by any persons by the authority, or the orders, or proclamations of the President, made as aforesaid, are hereby approved in all respects, legalized, and made valid to the same extent, and with the same effects, as if said orders and proclamations had been issued and made; and said arrests, imprisonments, proceedings, and acts had been done under the previous express authority and direction of the Congress of the United States, and in pursuance of a law thereof previously enacted, and expressly authorizing and directing the same to be done; and no civil court of the United States, or of any State, or of the District of Columbia, or of any District or Territory of the United States, shall have or take jurisdiction of, or in any manner reverse any of the proceedings had or acts done aforesaid; nor shall any person be held to answer in any of said courts for any act done or omitted to be done in pursuance of any of said proclamations or orders, or by authority or with the approval of the President, within the period aforesaid, respecting any of the matters aforesaid; *and all officers and other persons in the service of the United States, acting in the premises, shall be held primâ facie to have been authorized by the President;* and all acts or parts of acts inconsistent with the provisions hereof are hereby repealed."

it is, on the authority of decided cases, far the most unwarrantable instance, for the reason that it asserts a power to take away, at once and directly, a vested right of action.

It is to be feared that in Congress, at the present time, the success of party is paramount to all considerations respecting the integrity of the Constitution. With the dominant party the great subject of rejoicing is in the fact that the constitutional power of the President to check unconstitutional or improvident legislation is, for the time being, rendered inoperative by a party majority in Congress so strong that it can pass any measure which the party caucus shall dictate, over the veto. Constitutional objections on the part of the minority, to measures devised by the majority to secure a party ascendency, are treated with scorn, and a veto is a signal for passing with hot haste the measure which is objected to. The unprecedented course of refusing to print the message containing a veto, for the purpose of consideration, has been made recently the subject of party gratulation.[1]

Thus the two Houses of Congress exercise their legislative powers uninfluenced by the checks and balances which the Constitution intended to place in the hands of the President, or rather perhaps previously influenced to disregard them.

The great fear of party is not that the constitutional union of the States is endangered, and constitutional liberty imperrilled, but that there may be loss of office.

The great subject of party denunciation is the Executive. The great question is not whether the President is exercising

[1] Here is what was said of the passage of the District Suffrage Bill, a few days since, which certainly was not a measure that required indecent haste: —

"It was expected that the House would set its heel upon the veto immediately on its reception, and this expectation was not disappointed; for it was taken up and read as soon as it came from the Senate, and the bill was at once put on its passage. The Senate went a long step beyond its previous record regarding vetoes. The usual motion to lay on the table and print was made, but, to the astonishment of most spectators, and to the gratification of not a few, the chamber refused to delay action long enough for this purpose, and there, as well as subsequently in the House, the bill was at once put on its passage. The message has not yet been printed, and it seems likely enough that the future collector of old documents will search in vain through the files of the Senate for this paper. As if to guard against such a contingency, and with a possible instinctive perception of its coming fate, the President, establishing a new precedent, had it very handsomely printed and stitched before sending it to Congress. Curiosity shops wanting a copy of the first veto that was printed before delivery, are hereby notified that this is the document for which application should be made." — *Boston Daily Advertiser*.

his powers constitutionally, but whether he sticks to the party which elected him to office, in all measures which the leaders see fit to devise; and the impeachment which is threatened, is in fact based substantially upon his failure to follow the behests of the party. If he had but been ready to concur in all the extreme and unconstitutional measures of the party, we should have heard nothing of malversation in office.

In the course of denunciation nothing is too violent, nothing too gross. The political pulpit strives to come in for its share.

The Rev. Horatio Stebbins is reported to have made this utterance in a thanksgiving sermon, that is, in a partisan philippic, uttered in the pulpit, at San Francisco: —

"The most striking thing in Mr. Johnson's character is a feeling that he has no social position. Kicked, insulted, scorned, he has returned kicks, insults, and scorn. Not sure of himself, he is under the delusion of false estimation, and exposed to flattery and vanity. His education was among people with whom ribaldry and insolence were both argument and persuasion. A provincialism of mind which applies to the whole country the standards of his village, and to the times the old traditions of party, is his next defect. He is oblivious of the great change; he acts as if the people felt now as they did in 1860, when Douglas was telling them, no matter which, freedom or slavery, God or Devil. In turning people out of office to build up a party, he does not discern that the great republican party is in no proper sense a party — but the country itself. He calls Congress illegitimate, yet signs or vetoes its laws. He calls the States that elected him an unconstitutional Union, and yet claims to be president of the whole country."

This reverend gentleman must have attained, at least, to the degree of Doctor of Vituperative Theology, and exhibits himself as a fair specimen of the class of political clergymen who, commencing with a commendable sympathy for the slave, have ended in making their pulpits huckster shops for traffic in the small wares of partisan politics. Partisan papers circulate this as "a Portrait of the President."

But this reverend gentleman and others who, like him, prostitute their pulpits to the purposes of party, cannot carry away the palm of vituperation uncontested.

In a recent speech in the Senate of the United States the denunciation of the President was even more violent.

I shall not trouble you with a specimen of that part of the speech, but I wish to turn your attention to two other particulars of it. The senator said: —

"I know that the President sometimes quotes the Constitution, and professes to carry out its behests. But this is of little value. A French historian, whose fame as a writer is eclipsed by his greater fame as an orator, who had held important posts, and now in advancing years is still eminent in public life, has used words which aptly characterize an attempt like that of the President. I quote the history of M. Thiers: —

"'When any one wishes to make a revolution, or a counter revolution, it is necessary always to disguise the illegality as much as possible, and to this end to use the terms of the Constitution, in order to destroy it, and also the members of the government, in order to overturn it.'"

The senator's apparent unconsciousness that this language of Mons. Thiers is equally applicable to the majorities of the two Houses of Congress who, in all their unconstitutional acts and resolutions, make at least equal pretence that they are acting under the Constitution, may be regarded as somewhat remarkable.

In closing his speech the senator indulged himself in another quotation of some significance. He said: —

"But before I take my seat you will pardon me if I read a brief lesson which seems as if written for the hour. The words are as beautiful as emphatic.

"'The dogmas of the quiet past are inadequate to the stormy present. The occasion is piled high with difficulty and we must rise with the occasion. As our case is new, so we must think anew and act anew. We must disenthrall ourselves and then we shall save our country.'"

"These are the words of Abraham Lincoln. They are as full of vital force now as when he uttered them. I entreat you not to neglect the lesson. Learn from this how to save our country."

The dogmas of the quiet past, thus referred to, and which were originally, in time of war, said to be inadequate to the then stormy present, were those which related to the powers granted by the Constitution, and to the administration of the general government.

And the disenthrallment which is to be effected, and which is thus urged as the *lesson of the hour*, *long after the war is over;*

what is it? What thrall exists upon the two Houses of Congress which they are urged to burst? Not certainly one of courtesy to the President leading to an unwise sanction of his measures. Not one of deference to the opinion of political opponents, and consequent doubt and hesitation respecting measures proposed. Not one imposed by existing laws, for they can be repealed and others substituted. Not even one arising from the use of the veto, defeating the will of the majorities of both Houses in relation to such alterations, for the great reason of partisan rejoicing has been, and is, that this is no longer even a constitutional safeguard, those majorities being, as we have seen, so triumphant that they can pass anything the party dictates by a majority of two thirds, without even a respectful consideration of the objections of the President.

The only thrall which exists is the Constitution, and perhaps the judicial power under it. And the "lesson" of the "hour" was that the dominant party should reject the interpretations and constructions of it in the past, and rid themselves of the restraints imposed by it in the present. I regret to say that this is not thinking anew or acting anew. We have had much of this kind of thought and action within the last few years.

There are already significant utterances respecting the removal of the thrall of the judiciary, by some change of circuits which shall depose the majority of one, and exalt the minority of the court.

But a change of circuit will hardly answer the purpose. What measure is to be devised, and what "use" is to be next made of "the terms of the Constitution in order to destroy it," remains to be seen. The Supreme Court has recently been spoken of in the House as existing alone by the breath of Congress.

It was said by Mr. Chief Justice Chase in delivering the opinion of the minority of the court in Milligan's case, and when speaking of the asserted power of Congress, under the Constitution, in time of public danger, to provide for the organization of a military commission, and for trial by that commission, of persons engaged in an alleged conspiracy, "We have no apprehension that this power, under the American system of government, in which all official authority is derived from the people and exercised under direct responsibility to the people, is more likely to be abused than the power to regulate commerce, or the power to borrow money." This is certainly a most astonishing confidence. One can hardly refrain from an inquiry whether the confidence would be so strong in case the power happened to be lodged in an adverse political party.

But even when in the hands of political friends, is there no danger that it may be used to subserve the purposes of malice and revenge? Let the case of Smith, Brothers, give a most emphatic answer.

The interest of party can be subserved only remotely and indirectly by the exercise of the power to regulate commerce, or that to borrow money. The purposes of malice, and the gratification of a desire for revenge, not at all.

But, on the other hand, to what an indefinite extent party purposes can be promoted by the imprisonment of a political opponent! It was not the fault of the old police commissioners of Baltimore, or their subservient judge, that the imprisonment of their successors, on an allegation that they were disturbing the peace (to wit, by attempting to exercise their lawful authority), did not work out the success of their nefarious schemes for the political ascendency of their party. They undoubtedly supposed that they had thus made "a sure thing" of it.

Gentlemen of the Law School, — I have thus endeavored to present to you a true picture of the state of the country, for a few years past, in regard to its constitutional law.

I have, heretofore, attempted to show the danger to which civil liberty is subject, by the preponderance of executive power in time of war.

A part of my object, at the present time, is more particularly to exhibit the dangers of the preponderance of the legislative department, in engrossing the powers of the other departments, in time of peace.

I am aware of the spirit of progress which listens to the lessons of history, and the counsels of experience, with impatience; and of the self-confidence which prefers its own judgment, above all arguments and reasons, and disregards all consequences in the pursuit of a favorite object. Some lawyers in Congress have sunk their constitutional law in their adherence to party. Others, outside of that body, have let their indignation against the rebellion run away with it.

Let me urge upon you, gentlemen, a careful study of the past, — of "the dead past," — to use the favorite phraseology of those who reject its warnings. Let me remind you that what men have been, men may be, and will be again. Let me say that ambition seeking power and place, unscrupulous in its measures for the attainment of its object, and regardless of consequences so that object is attained, is as active and enterprising now, as it has been in any period of the history of the world. Let me suggest that sophistry is none the less specious in the law than it is in religion, where false prophets and false apostles deceive even the very elect. Let me warn you that the liberties of the country have no immunity from peril and wreck, and that there is no policy of insurance upon which indemnity can be sought when the loss shall have come.

Be it yours, gentlemen, without regard to the transitory interests of the hour, or the excited passions of the hour, to exhibit a steadfast, unswerving adherence to the principles of civil liberty, secured, it was fondly hoped, by the constitutions of the States and of the United States. And rest assured that these principles are to be preserved only by a firm and unflinching maintenance of the great divisions of political power in separate, and to a great extent, independent departments of government; and by the preservation of the State and the National governments, confining oach to its proper sphere of action and of duty, within its constitutional limits.

LECTURE II.

THE ORIGIN OF THE UNITED STATES, AND THE LEGAL STATUS OF THE SOUTHERN STATES ON THE SUPPRESSION OF THE REBELLION.

Delivered in Dartmouth College, April, 1869.

THERE are two theories in relation to the Constitution of the United States, which not only differ widely in reference to its origin, and the powers which exist under it, but which may lead to very different results in regard to its amendment.

According to one of them, the Constitution was formed by a convention of delegates from the several States, and adopted by the people of the several States, acting separately, and surrendering thereby a portion of the powers of the States, and of the people of the States, to the new government created by the Constitution; by means of which agreement and surrender, the people of the United States came into existence as an entire people, and became a nation for the purposes mentioned in the Constitution; all the powers not thereby granted, or incidental to those granted, remaining with the States, and the people of the States as such.

The other theory is based upon the position, that the people of the United States became a nation upon the declaration of independence, and that as such nation the whole people framed and adopted the Constitution of the United States, granting to the States, and to the people of the States, rights of representation in the new government under the Constitution; and, that all powers not granted to the government of the United States, or recognized by the Constitution as belonging to the States, remain in the whole people, and not in the several peoples of the different States.

A very elaborate attempt to sustain the right of Congress to reconstruct the States where acts of secession were passed, is based, to a considerable extent, upon the latter of these theories.[1] And the argument of the author may serve as a convenient text for an examination of these adverse theories, with a view to ascertain the origin of the government of the United States, and the status of the Southern States on the suppression of the rebellion. The author was a lawyer of eminence in his day, prone, however, to persuade himself of the truth of that which he desired to believe. If it shall be found, on examination, that his positions are not sustained by the facts, and that he persuaded himself of the correctness of the theory which he supported, upon insufficient evidence, not only will his conclusions fall, but we shall have *primâ facie* evidence, at least, that the theory itself is indefensible.

Repudiating the question whether those States, by reason of the rebellion of their inhabitants, were to be accounted as in or out of the Union, because no such question has arisen upon the facts, the author says: —

"They, during and after the rebellion, were States in possession of defined territories, and under organized governments, to which they professed allegiance. And they were clearly in the Union in so far as their territories, people, and amenability to the Constitution and laws of the Union are concerned. The National government still maintained its right of territorial jurisdiction over them, and of enforcing obedience to the Constitution and laws as fully as it ever had; and their inhabitants remained citizens of the Union, and entitled to all the civil and political rights and immunities which they ever possessed as such, excepting those which they had forfeited, or lost, or abandoned by their treason."

"By that treason each inhabitant has forfeited his liberty and life as the penalty of his crime, if the government shall see fit to exact it by due process of law; but until arrest, and sentence, and such conviction, he is still entitled to protection and immunity, and the enjoyment of all the civil rights which he ever had resulting from such merely individual citizenship." — "And he may be restored to the future undisturbed enjoyment of them by an act of amnesty of the General Government, or by a pardon from the Executive after conviction and sentence."

The theories which would dissolve the Union by reducing

1 "*Reconstruction.* Claims of the Inhabitants of the States engaged in the Rebellion to Restoration of Political Rights and Privileges under the Constitution. By Charles G. Loring. Boston: Little, Brown & Company. 1866."

the Southern States to a territorial condition, through State suicide, or conquest, as in the case of foreign war, or through the provision of the Constitution guaranteeing to each State a republican form of government, are thus exploded; and the epigrammatic assertion that "rebels have no rights, except a right to be hanged," is distinctly negatived, — as their right to be hanged, and of course their duty to be hanged, arises only upon conviction and judgment.

"But," the author says further, "with regard to the political rights of the inhabitants of a State in its corporate political capacity, — *those of representation in the House and Senate for instance*, — these" "do not rest upon nor result from their individual citizenship, as citizens of the United States merely; but depend also upon the political relations which the State bears to the Union, and cease to exist whenever it has suspended, lost, forfeited, or abandoned the rights belonging to it as a state in its normal relations to the government, and can be restored only by restoration of the State to those relations."

He asserts the forfeiture of the political rights of the inhabitants of the Southern States, and the right of the General Government to prescribe the conditions upon which they may be restored to equal political privileges with the other States, as consequences resulting from the war, and upon several other grounds, which I propose to consider at this time, hoping that this may be the last of these unconstitutional theories respecting the *status* of the Southern States, which it will be my duty to examine and refute.

This forfeiture is first attempted to be maintained, under the power to make war. The author says: —

"Upon looking into the Constitution, it is found to contain, among others, the following express provisions, applying exclusively to the States in their political corporate capacities as such; namely: The United States shall guarantee to every State in the Union a republican form of government." "No State shall enter into any treaty, or alliance, or confederation," or "enter into any agreement or compact with another State, or with any foreign power." "The citizens of each State shall be entitled to all the privileges and immunities of [citizens in] the several States." "The Constitution and the laws of the United States which shall be made in pursuance thereof, shall be the supreme law of the land," and then quoting the provisions that the President shall take care that the laws be faithfully executed, and that Congress shall have power to provide for calling forth the militia to execute the laws, he inquires whether "in the face of these provisions it is possible to believe that any one State may at pleasure impose a despotic or monarchical government upon an unwilling and oppressed portion of its people;" and so, whether the States may violate the other provisions above cited, — arriving at the conclusion that for such violations "it is obvious that war is the only remedy;" that "any effective denial or violations of these provisions of the Constitution by any State, must be by forcible resistance of the lawful officers of the United States, civil or military, engaged in the duty of compelling compliance with them;" "and if such forcible resistance be resorted to by a State, the case presented becomes at once that of an organized government, possessing territorial jurisdiction, and asserting sovereignty and independence internal and external, and claiming the personal allegiance of its citizens as paramount to all other allegiance, taking up arms to repel the attempt of another sovereign State to enforce obedience to its asserted authority; and this is nothing less than actual war, civil war indeed, but none the less actual war between sovereign States, or those claiming to be such, and attended with all the attributes and consequences of war according to the public law, or law of nations."

Then he says, that

"One of the best established principles of that code is, that as there is no acknowledged arbiter to judge between the parties engaged in war, the victor has of necessity the right to dictate the terms of peace, provided that they be not inconsistent with humanity and the generally recognized principles of that code. And this rule, under certain limitations, is as applicable to a civil war as to one between sovereign States of no antecedent connections with each other." And thereupon he cites Vattel, and Wheaton upon the Law of Nations, Dana's ed. § 296, and the Prize Cases, 2 Black's Sup. C. Rep. 638, and concludes, that as the judgment of war was against the confederate States, a "just right accrued to the United States, not only to enforce obedience to the duties imposed by the Constitution, and keep the confederate States under military control until the peaceful fulfilment of them could be relied upon; but also to require full indemnity for the wrongs and losses caused by the rebellion, including payment of the debt incurred in suppressing it, if the confederate States could reimburse the amount of it, and any security which reason and justice might show to be necessary to prevent any future perpetration of the crime."

I have given extended extracts, that the learned writer may have the full benefit of his positions, and now I have to say, in the first place, in general terms, that his argument is all wrong. His conclusion shows that the Union and the Constitution would be broken up, and the confederate States held as a conquered province; which is not under, but outside of the Constitution, and in entire conflict with it.

The law of nations has nothing to do with a civil war as between the parties themselves, unless, perhaps, in the application of the law of prize. That law governs the relation which exists between the parties to a civil war and other nations who recognize the existence of that war and the parties as belligerents. But as between the parties themselves, — the government assailed on the one hand, and the insurgents on the other, — the law of nations has no application. The acts of the insurgents are treason, and may be punished as such under the municipal law, which, if the war was like a foreign war, could not be done. The war may assume large proportions, to such extent that the government may find it expedient not to punish the treason. The insurgents may be successful, and then there is revolution.

But the argument and conclusion of the writer fail for other reasons. While the law of nations does not govern such a case of war, as between the parties to it, the Constitution of the United States makes no provision for a war between the United States and one of the States, whether begun by one or the other of the parties. It not only contemplates no such case, but such a war is entirely impossible as long as the union of the people and of the States exists under the Constitution. With a revolution which severs a State from the Union, war between such State and the General Government becomes at once a possibility. Secession, if admitted to be effectual, would make it possible. But until there is revolution to the extent of the severance of a State from the Union, so that treason is no longer committed by acts of hostility, the State cannot lift its armed hand against the Union, nor the Union set its armed heel upon a State. This results from the fact that by the Constitution, and for the purposes of the Constitution, the people of the United States became one people, — an entire nation. Such a war, therefore, would be the warring of a nation against itself, and we are taught that even the kingdom of Satan cannot stand under such a warfare. Such a war would of itself be dissolution, — disintegration. For the purposes of war against each other, no such division as State and United States, territorial or otherwise, exists. All attempts to array a State against the General Government in war, are personally criminal, and the party is answerable personally for his offence ; but he is not, and cannot be, authorized to act for the State, and it is not, therefore, the treason of the State, or the war of the State, while the State exists in the Union.

It is quite true that there may be unlawful acts, treason itself, under semblance of State authority, by a usurpation of State offices, and the unlawful appropriation of the property and resources of the State. A majority of the people of a State might by possibility attempt to set up a monarchical government. It would be a very poor relief to the oppressed minority if the remedy was to be (as held by this writer) a war against the State, involving the minority equally with the majority in its horrors.

But it may be asked, what is the remedy other than war against the State. Certainly a very complete one, having for its object the overthrow of the unlawful government (which would not and could not be the government of a State within the Union), and the punishment of the offenders, personally ; not the deprivation of the rights of the State, or its subjection to pains, penalties, or bonds for good behavior. So far from that, the United States is, by the clause which has been cited, bound to guarantee, to that very State, a republican form of government, — to protect that State against such crimes, even of its own people. Is the United States under this clause of obligation to protect the State, to turn round upon it, make war upon it, and punish the State itself, to deprive it of its rights, and destroy its equality with the other States ? The thing would be preposterous. The United States is, of course, clothed with authority to pass laws which will enable that government to keep its covenant, — laws for the punishment of every one who should assume the office of king, or do any other act under such pretended monarchy. True, again, it might be necessary to enforce the laws by military authority, and this, if the criminals were strong enough, might lead to a war, a civil war. But it would be a war against the monarchists,— the insurgents,— who may have organized, claiming to be a state, or a confederacy, or a nation. A recognition of the insurgents as a belligerent party by England, France, and Spain, and all the other powers of Europe, with the King of Dahomey added, would not alter the character of such a war, from that of a treasonable war of persons, to a war of a State against the United States, nor give authority to the United States to conquer or punish the State. The victory would be one over persons, over the unlawful organization, and not over a part of the nation itself.

And so in relation to the other clauses of the Constitution by which States may not make treaties, &c., &c. What the State is thus inhibited from doing, the State cannot do. The prohibition creates an absolute disability. Individuals may violate this provision, in the name of the State, and be personally responsible for their misdeeds. But the attempted treaty or other prohibited act is wholly void, so far as the United States is concerned. Of course it is not the act of the State.

It may not be amiss here to consider this clause of guaranty in another aspect, in which it presents itself in this connection. I have shown (upon another occasion) how it came into the Constitution, why it was inserted, and what is its true construction.[1]

It is, as we readily perceive, a covenant of protection on the part of the United States, — protection to the oppressed minority, protection to the other States, — a duty assumed by the United States. But suppose the United States should not keep this covenant. The Constitution and laws of the United States are the supreme law of the land. The President shall take care that the laws be faithfully executed. Congress shall have power for calling forth the militia to execute the laws, says this writer. All very true. There is power enough. But the President cannot subvert this monarchical government without some action of Congress; and suppose the majority in Congress, believing that the subversion of the monarchy will not be the means of gaining votes for the party in the next presidential election, think that it is not best, therefore, to interfere, does

[1] *Revolution and Reconstruction*, Lecture II.

nothing, and so no war is made upon the monarchical organization called a State. The United States is then in the wrong. What is the remedy? If war by the United States against the State is the proper remedy for the violation of the duty on the part of the State to maintain a republican government, which duty is not expressed but implied in this clause, why is not war upon the United States by the State, which certainly has an interest in having this express covenant kept, the proper remedy to enforce it. If it be thought that here would be a little practical difficulty, inasmuch as such a war must necessarily be waged by the "oppressed minority," not only against the United States, but against the majority of monarchists, who caused the offence, that difficulty would not exist in reference to a war against the United States by the other States, which certainly have also an interest in having this covenant kept and this duty performed. War against the United States for a violation of duty is just as proper as war against a State for such a violation.

The argument of this and other writers, in reference to this clause of guaranty, leads fairly to the inquiry respecting the mode of its enforcement; and I have run out the argument to show the absurdity of any conclusion that war upon a State is the remedy, in any case, for a violation, by the majority of the people of a State, of the constitutional obligations of the State. If the majority of the people of a State should refuse to choose senators, or to elect representatives in Congress, and should thus, at the same time, abandon a privilege and violate a duty, we should say, in common parlance, that the State was guilty; and yet it would not be the act of the State, which, as a State in the Union, can only act lawfully. It would be the unauthorized act of individuals, and war upon the State would not be the remedy.

It may be found to be true that while there is power in the United States, — through statutes, which being the supreme law may be enforced by judicial or executive power exerted against individuals, — to enforce all the duties of the States, there is no such sanction in respect to the duties of the United States, — the reliance for the performance of those duties being upon the virtue and patriotism of those who are intrusted by the people with their performance. If that fails, the evil must be endured until the people apply the remedy. There can be no indictment or impeachment of a majority in Congress, nor any war upon that body, nor upon the United States and the Constitution. And there is just as little foundation, under and within the Constitution, for war upon a State, although the treason of individuals may reach to such a magnitude of organization, as that there may be war upon them.

The author next undertakes to maintain his notion of "the right of the General Government to prescribe the conditions upon which the inhabitants of the rebel States may be restored to equal political privileges with the other States under the Constitution, independently of the right resulting from war," and says "there are several other grounds upon which, as is believed, it may be satisfactorily vindicated."

The first proposition which he then suggests is, "that the power of deciding upon the right of such restoration, and upon the terms of it, resides in the General Government as matter of absolute and inevitable necessity."

This is put as if the States could not be restored, except by some action of the General Government. But such a proposition has no foundation in fact nor in law. If, on the close of the war, the United States had withdrawn all the troops, and left the peoples of those States to reorganize their governments, under the State constitutions, as they existed before the war, and the inhabitants had proceeded, upon such notice as was satisfactory to them, to hold primary meetings, and to elect members of the State legislatures, and then to elect senators and representatives in Congress, those senators and representatives would have been admitted to their seats, and the "restoration" would have been complete, without any measures of reconstruction by Congress.

The presidential plan, devised, it is said by Mr. Lincoln, and followed by Mr. Johnson, of appointing military governors; and through that mode, by means of the action of such governors, taking measures for reorganization, would have accomplished the same thing, without any terms or conditions prescribed. That mode gave an opportunity to require, through the military organization, the abolition of slavery, as terms of restoration, not from necessity, but from choice.

The abolition of slavery alone, however, it was feared, would not secure the ascendency of the party in power, and to secure that, came the "*necessity*" that the majority in Congress should impose such terms as would accomplish that object, and hence the "absolute and inevitable necessity" that the power of deciding upon the rights of restoration and its terms, should reside in the General Government. The necessity was the one described by Mr. Patterson, candidate for Congress, when he pledged himself "to support any military necessity to which the administration *should see fit to resort.*" That describes the inevitable necessity exactly. It is a necessity which the party chooses, creates, adopts, resorts to, and which exists only by such choice and adoption. We have all heard of the man who was "forced to go a volunteer." I think we have his counterpart in the man who voluntarily imposes upon himself a present inevitable necessity.

Necessity has been long denounced as the tyrant's plea; and the use which has been made of the term, in this connection, shows that this description of it is an apt one. *The Constitution recognizes no necessity to do anything which it does not authorize to be done. Especially, it recognizes no necessity to destroy the rights which it solemnly guarantees.*

"The next proposition," he says, "is, that State rights being corporate rights, or privileges, or franchises only, belonging to the States as subjects of the National Government, and being lost or forfeited by their rebellion against it, never could revert or be recovered by their subjugation or submission; but any restoration of them must be by a grant from the sovereign power which created them."

"*State rights and powers are such, and such only, as were granted, defined, or recognized by the Constitution.* The States are in no sense sovereign under it, nor are they in any part of it styled or recognized to be such. They have no right to decide any question under it in the last resort; but are always amenable and subject to the final decision of the General Government upon it."

This last is certainly a very strange position, unless there is more special pleading here than is apparent upon the face of it. It may be said that all State rights and powers are "recognized" by the Constitution, in the tenth amendment, which provides that "the powers not delegated to the United States by the Constitution, nor prohibited by it to the States, are reserved to the States respectively, or to the people," which is merely an explicit declaration of that which would have been true without any such declaration. It was adopted to remove fears, and place the matter, as it was supposed, beyond cavil.

But this provision which thus "recognizes" the rights of the States, neither grants, nor defines them. Nor are they "granted" elsewhere in the Constitution of the United States, nor "defined" to any great extent. The Constitution deals in prohibitions upon the States to exercise, in the future, rights of a sovereign character which they had exercised before, and might have continued to exercise but for the surrender of them, through the adoption of the Constitution.

Again, — It is not true, that the States "have no right to decide any question under it [the Constitution] in the last resort," even in a limited sense, for the validity of the laws of Congress, and the question of the rightful exercise of power under such laws, may be drawn in question in the State courts, and if the decision of such court is in favor of the validity of the statute or power, the State court is one of the last resort, and the decision final. It is only when the validity of a treaty or statute of, or an authority exercised under, the United States, is drawn in question, and the decision is against their validity, or where the validity of a statute of, or an authority exercised under, a State, is drawn in question on the ground of their being repugnant to the Constitution, treaties, or laws of the United States, and the decision is in favor of the validity of the State statute or authority, or where there is a decision against a title, right, privilege, or exemption claimed under the United States, that appeal or error lies from the State courts.

It may be said that the decision of the State court is thus final, in questions regarding the Constitution, treaties, and laws of the United States, not by any provision of the Constitution, but because Congress has not seen fit to provide for an appeal from the State court, except in the cases enumerated. Perhaps this is so. If it be, it will serve to show that the States have the right to decide all questions in the last resort, except when the right is taken away by or under the Constitution. If, however, it be intended to confine the assertion to those questions only which arise "under the Constitution," and are not reached by any statute, it is a special averment which fails to support the general doctrine, for the United States, being a limited government, and the powers conferred upon its several departments limited powers, there is a vast variety of questions which the States, and the courts of the States, decide in the last resort, not by any grant from the General Government, but by virtue of their original sovereignty, which has thus far never been surrendered or taken away. It was because the States were not willing to part with a sovereign right, that the eleventh amendment to the Constitution provided that "the judicial power of the United States shall not be construed to extend to any suit in law or in equity, commenced or prosecuted against one of the United States by citizens of another State, or by citizens or subjects of any foreign power.

That the States are bound by the Constitution of the United States, and by laws duly passed in pursuance of it, is undoubtedly true. But that they are "subjects" of the United States in any ordinary sense of the term "subjects," as used in describing political or civil rights, is not true.

The next assertion under the proposition which we are considering is that "the right of representation in Congress and so to participate in the administration of the General Government, was not one belonging to them [the States] in their original capacities when the Constitution was framed, nor one created by them as the framers of the Constitution. It was one conferred upon and granted to them by the whole people of the United States, in the formation of that frame or structure of the government." "*The people of the United States was the grantor, and the several States respectively were the grantees of that right.*"

And so he reaches the conclusion, that these rights are mere corporate rights, belonging to the States only as political corporations or societies; and he perceives not why they may not be lost and forfeited by misuser or nonuser in the same manner as may be any other corporate rights created by the general government "from which they were derived."

This position is certainly more astonishing, if possible, than the last. The author admits that "the nature of the political relations of the several States to the United States is obviously pure matter of law," and that "any question concerning the violation or forfeiture of them, or the right of restoration to them, if lost or forfeited, is also a pure question of law."

Now, as a pure question of law, how could the people of the

United States make a grant of political rights, or corporate rights, or any other rights, before they came into existence as "the people of the United States?" We might as well say that a child created itself and at the instant of its birth granted to its mother the right to nurse it. "The people of the United States," in order to make a grant, must first have a political existence as a people, and there was no such people or government until the adoption of the Constitution, which was the creation of the peoples of the several States.

It is enough to say in answer to this position "that the General Government is the grantor, and the States the grantees of the right of representation in Congress," that the thing is an utter impossibility, consistently with the history of the formation of the Constitution, under which, and only under which, this right of representation exists. It is true, as the author says, that "the right of representation in Congress, and so to participate in the administration of the General Government, was not one belonging to them [the States] in their original capacities when [that is, before] the Constitution was formed." They could not, in their original capacities, have a right of representation in a congress under the Constitution, when there was no provision for a constitution, and of course no congress under it. But it is not true, as he represents, that the right was not one created by the States, or rather by the peoples of the States, "as the framers of the Constitution."

The General Government could not be organized until this right of representation had been exercised by the peoples of the States, and by the States, as such, in the election of representatives and senators in a congress to be formed; and this was the first act of the organization which brought "the people of the United States" into existence, as a whole people, for certain limited purposes, under the Constitution. "We, the people of the United States," uttered their first words in the preamble to the Constitution which made them "we the people," and of course did not utter them until that Constitution became operative through ratifications by the peoples of the several States.

The formation of the government of the United States, — the formation of this nation, — was, throughout, the several action of the populations of the States. The States, acting severally, sent delegates to the convention which devised the scheme of a national government, — the scheme of a nation to be organized under a constitution which should create that nation. The Constitution which these State delegates framed was submitted to the peoples of the States severally. The acts of the peoples of the several States, acting separately through conventions called by their respective State legislatures, ratified the Constitution. The ratification of the people of New Hampshire, the ninth State ratifying, secured its adoption. These ratifications gave existence to the Constitution, and thereby life to the nation. Through them came authority, by a provision of the Constitution which was thus adopted, for the election of senators and representatives in Congress, by the several States, before the organization of the government of the United States, and for the purpose of organizing that government, — and of course before the United States existed as a government under the Constitution.

These elections by the peoples of the States respectively, were not, therefore, and could not have been, by any grant of the United States, for the United States spoke only through the action of the peoples of the States. The government of the United States received the breath of life, and power and right from them, by that instrument; and it would be absurd to hold that by the same instrument by which the people of the United States, as an entire people, came into existence, and at the instant when they came into existence, they made a grant of power to their creators, to perfect that existence.

All elections of senators and representatives since have the same original foundation. Until the Constitution went into operation the people of the country collectively had no power to make any grant. It went into operation for the purpose of the elections necessary to organize the government, by means of the ratifications; but it was not operative for any other purpose than these elections, until the government was organized. The Constitution gives no power to make a grant of a right of representation either expressly or by implication. There can be no *construction* by which it is *presumed* or assumed that the people of the United States came into existence as a nation and then made the grant of a right of representation. There are cases in which it has been presumed, for the purpose of giving effect to what was intended as a grant, that a corporation made the grant the instant itself came into existence. *But there is no case in which it was ever presumed that a corporation granted its own charter, and therein provided for its own organization by conferring the power necessary for that purpose.* A legal presumption therefore that the United States granted the right to choose the senators and representatives who were chosen before the government was fully born and who assisted at its birth, is neither a presumption of fact nor of law, but against both.

The next ground upon which this author contends that the political rights may be accounted as forfeited and lost is, that having been granted "upon condition of the continued existence of certain prescribed relations to the United States and obedience to the Constitution and the laws; and that condition having been voluntarily and entirely broken, they were by the terms of the grant, and the principle universally recognized in continuing grants upon conditions, totally and irrecoverably forfeited and lost."

It is only necessary to say upon this point that the supposition of a grant from the General Government entirely failing, any implication of a condition annexed to it, such as is mentioned, fails with it. We need not discuss the question, therefore, whether if there had been such a grant there could have been an implication of such a condition.

But it may be remarked that alleged forfeitures of grants upon condition are subjects for judicial determination. A forfeiture of corporate rights through misuser and nonuser, is not to be declared and made effectual by any declaration of the legislative department of the government; but, upon the ordinary principles of law, is to be made the subject of judicial inquiry. For the same reason the right of the two Houses of Congress to judge of the election of their own members would not cover the case. If these rights were corporate rights, and the General Government alleges such a forfeiture, then upon the admission of the author that any question concerning the violation or forfeiture of them is also a pure question of law, we must have a process of *quo warranto*, by the Attorney-General, filed in the Supreme Court, and the States must be required to come in and show by what authority they still assume to exercise such rights of representation. Such a process would surely be a novelty as well as an absurdity. But to such ends we come at last, on this reasoning.

But the author says: —

"There is another and a broader view to be taken of this subject, in the light of the great principles upon which the Constitution was founded, and the great purposes for which it was created, extending far beyond any merely literal or technical rules of construction as applied to written contracts or instruments in the ordinary business of life."

He says: —

"The foundation principles of self-preservation and of essential security for the great objects of the compact must have controlling influence over all other principles, if in conflict with them, when applied to any issue in which they are involved. The principle of self-preservation is fully recognized as one of established law in all civilized communities."

Between the two paragraphs just quoted are these assertions:

"*The nation*, as history abundantly shows, *existed as a nation before the Constitution was formed.* The nation created the Constitution, not the Constitution the nation. It constructed that national compact for the more perfect definition and distribution of the various rights and powers which its citizens possessed, or were intended to possess, in their individual capacities and in their corporate capacities as States," etc.

Again: —

"The government formed by the Constitution represents the nation in everything pertaining to it as a nation. Its life is the life of the nation. And it not only has the right, but is, on every principle of duty, bound to protect that life at all costs and all hazards; and for that end to exercise other powers than those expressly given by the Constitution, if manifestly necessary for that end, upon the obvious principle that the possession of such ultimate power of self-preservation was necessarily implied in its creation."

The assertion that "the nation existed as a nation before the Constitution was formed" he makes emphatic by italics.

Let us go back and inquire further of history as to the truth of this allegation.

By the term "*nation*" in this connection is evidently meant the people of the whole country as an entire community contradistinguished from the people of the several States, and having as such community rights and powers of a political character; and the assertion is in effect that this entire community constructed this national compact. The whole scope of the argument shows this. To give the language any other construction would make it absurd, for this supposed nation it seems had citizens, and it constructed this national compact for the more perfect definition and distribution of the various rights and powers which those citizens possessed, or were intended to possess, in their individual capacities and in their corporate capacities as States.

Now veritable well known history gives a complete and emphatic denial to this whole proposition. History presents us in the first place thirteen colonies, under the common jurisdiction of Great Britain, but organized under separate charters, grants, and commissions; with their separate legislative, judicial, and executive departments, as completely independent of each other as any foreign nations, — with the exception of their common dependence upon the mother country, and in some instances a common governor. It shows a claim by Great Britain of a right to tax these colonies, which had no representation in the British Parliament, and a denial of that right, — a matter in which the colonies had a common interest only as the principle was asserted as to all, and each, and if acquiesced in would in the end be made operative in each. Then came the attempt to enforce the asserted right in one of these colonies and resistance there, — the sympathy of the others, the resolution to make a common cause in the assertion of the denial, as no one could maintain the controversy alone, and without union in making the resistance the claim would be enforced in detail against all. Then a Congress of Delegates appointed by each to consider the dangers common to all, to devise concert of action, and the recommendation of measures to be adopted by all, — acting separately, however, in the adoption of such measures. Then there is the armed attempt to enforce the measures of the crown, and the armed resistance directed by this Congress of Delegates, who, by the authority of popular organizations in the several colonies, appoint a Commander-in-Chief and do divers other things necessary to be done in the prosecution of the warfare, but nothing which might not be done by deputies of different populations, assembled with authority for the purpose. Connected with all this are earnest protestations of loyalty and of a desire only for redress of grievances, and that they do not desire to sever their connection as colonies with the mother country.

As the contest is prolonged, the probability of obtaining redress becomes less, the dangers of subjugation become more apparent, and the idea of independence is entertained. The several popular organizations discuss it, act upon it, and assent that it shall be declared. But it is the independence of the several colonies, which are to become free and independent States.

The nature and character of what was proposed to be done was well expressed by the action of the Connecticut Assembly, instructing its delegates to propose to Congress "to declare the United American Colonies free and independent States," and that they move and promote a plan of union and confederation of the colonies for the security and just preservation of their just rights and liberties, and for mutual defence and security, *saving that the administration of government and the power of forming governments for, and the regulation of the internal police of each colony ought to be left and remain to the respective colonial legislatures, and also that such plan of confederation be laid before such respective legislatures for their previous consideration and assent.*"

The Declaration of Independence is made by the delegates representing their respective constituents in accordance with the authority thus conferred, and it is, not that the whole people are an independent nation, nor with any assertion of a common power except as it is derived from their separate populations, but with a recital of grievances common to and affecting all, and with the distinct and emphatic declaration that these colonies "are, and of right ought to be, free and independent States." The assertion of independent sovereignty in each is thus made plain and explicit.

We cannot ignore the effect of these proceedings, and say that from the time Congress assembled there was a nation embracing the whole people; the people of the several colonies meanwhile professing their desire to remain separate colonies of Great Britain. The idea would be preposterous. But there was no change of organization or grant of power to Congress altering the constitution of that body, from its first organization to the Declaration. Congress in making the Declaration represented the people of the several colonies as distinct populations, as it represented those several populations when it first commenced its sessions, and it is beyond cavil (no, not beyond that, but beyond a reasonable doubt), that the language of the Declaration of Independence does not authorize any construction or interpretation of that instrument by which it can be made to assert the existence of any entire nation, arising out of the separation of the colonies from the mother country. Congress after the Declaration differed from its first organization only in this, that the delegates severally represented independent States instead of revolted colonies. The subsequent appointment of delegates was an exercise of the sovereignty which the Declaration asserted, — sovereignty in the several States.

Congress repeatedly recognized the sovereignty of the States.[1] There was in fact nothing else which could be sovereign. Congress was without the powers of a nation and could in no sense be sovereign, and there was nothing besides but the States. There was no allegiance due to Congress, — no treason against it. But the allegiance was to the several States, and treason was an offence against each accordingly. There were no citizens of the United States. The lack of power in Congress led to the formation of the Articles of Confederation, which as we have seen by the action of the Connecticut Assembly were contemplated when independence should be declared. The second of these articles, as they were drawn up by Congress and submitted to the several States, was in these words:

"Article 2d. Each State retains its sovereignty, freedom, and independence, and every power, jurisdiction, and right which is not by this confederation expressly delegated to the United States in Congress assembled."

1 The committee appointed to prepare a circular letter to accompany the Articles of Confederation, brought in the following draught: —

"In Congress, York Town, November 17th, 1777.

"Congress having agreed upon a plan of confederacy for securing the freedom, sovereignty, and independence of the United States, authentic copies are now transmitted for the consideration of the respective legislatures." . . . . . "Permit us then earnestly to recommend these articles to the immediate and dispassionate attention of the legislatures of the respective States. Let them be candidly reviewed under a sense of the difficulty of combining in one general system the various sentiments and interests of a continent divided into so many sovereign and independent communities, under a conviction of the absolute necessity of uniting all our councils and all our strength to maintain and defend our common liberties." *Journal*, 1777, pp. 513, 514.

Requiring the adoption of all the States, and Maryland objecting, because there was no provision respecting the public lands, they did not go into effect until her assent in 1781, and the States were of course sovereign up to that time, for the plain reason that up to that time they retained the sovereignty which the 2d Article admitted that they possessed.

Even after the adoption of the articles, although the States had thereby parted with some of the powers of sovereignty, Congress was not a nation, nor were the States, thus confederated, a nation. There was no power under the articles to institute a national executive or legislature. Congress possessed some powers of each character. But there was still no allegiance due to Congress or to the confederacy, nor any treason against Congress or the confederacy. Congress still admitted the sovereignty of the States.[1]

It was the insufficiency of the powers of the confederacy that caused the convention which framed the Constitution. The first idea of a national legislature, judiciary and executive, is found in a letter of Mr. Madison to Governor Randolph, after the convention was called; and the first movement towards the creation of a nation was in the resolution proposed by Governor Randolph in the convention. The Constitution, as framed, proposed the creation of a national life for certain limited purposes only.[2]

[1] In Congress, Aug. 12, 1782. "On the report of a committee, consisting of Mr. Lowell, Mr. Cornell, and Mr. Madison, to whom was referred a letter of the 9th of July, from the Commander-in-Chief, with sundry papers inclosed: —

"*Resolved*, That Congress approve the conduct of General Washington, in refusing to enter into any discussion with General Carleton on the subject of the treason laws passed by the several States.

"*Resolved*, That the States of America which compose the Union, being sovereign and independent, the laws respectively passed by them for their internal government and the punishment of their offending citizens, cannot be submitted to the discussion of a foreign power, much less of an enemy." — *Journals of Congress*, 1781–82, p. 436.

The report of the committee in favor of the admission of Vermont into the confederacy proposed, "That the district or territory called Vermont, as defined and limited in the resolutions of Congress of the 20th and 21st of August, 1781, be and it is hereby recognized and acknowledged by the name of the State of Vermont, as free, sovereign, and independent; and that a committee be appointed to treat and confer with the agents and delegates from said State, upon the terms and mode of the admission of the said State into the Federal Union." — *Journal*, 1781–82, p. 343.

[2] A friend who was somewhat inclined to this heresy of the existence of an entire nation from the Declaration of Independence, after a short discussion which appeared to convince him that the proposition was untenable, said to me, "Well, there was a sentiment of nationality from the first." The reply was, "You have hit it precisely." There was a *sentiment of nationality*. It was but a sentiment, until the adoption of

Having thus ascertained that the nation of the United States did not, and could not, under the circumstances, exist anterior to the Constitution, that the Constitution was framed by the peoples of the several States, and that these several populations, acting separately through the instrumentality of the Constitution, formed the nation; and, moreover, that this nation thus formed is a sovereignty only for particular and limited purposes, the States existing as perfect sovereignties from the time of the Declaration of Independence until they themselves, by their voluntary acts, parted with portions of their sovereignty, retaining the rest; and that these sovereignties would exist and be competent to act as perfect sovereignties if the nation under the Constitution of the United States should be destroyed, — we may well question the soundness of the proposition, that this nation of limited powers has any right to exercise any powers other than those granted, even for its own preservation. All powers not delegated to it expressly, or by implication, are retained by the States and the people. There is no grant of power to go outside of the Constitution for any purpose, not even for self-preservation. There is no power of that character incident to any of the powers granted. All incidental powers, or powers by implication, are inside and under the Constitution, and not outside of it. It is not "bound to protect its life at all costs, and all hazards." *It is not authorized to protect its life at the cost of the life of the States, or the liberties of the citizens of the several States.* To do so would be to pervert the purposes of its creation, — would be flagrant usurpation, which any State might lawfully resist for its own preservation, and so might come revolution.

But let us consider the proposition respecting the right of self-preservation a little farther, and assume, for the sake of the argument, that there is, incidental to the powers granted, an implied power in the nation of the United States, of self-preservation, and that it is bound to protect its life at all the costs and

the Constitution. There was a common sympathy arising from the common perils; and common rejoicings when they were surmounted. There was a feeling of common interest in the maintenance of the independence which had been achieved, — a desire for the strength to be found in united action, — an agreement to join in consultation, and in certain measures in relation to foreign intercourse. There was confederation, and powers conferred on Congress. But nationality consisted only in sentiment, not in fact.

hazards which may result consistently with the Constitution itself. We cannot say which are inconsistent with it. On this principle the result is the same. The nation cannot go outside of the Constitution by which it was created, and exercise powers not incident to the powers granted by the Constitution, and at costs and hazards which the Constitution does not justify. There can be no such incidental powers.

The principle of self-preservation, then, is to preserve itself in its constitutional form, — to save to itself the powers which it possesses, as those powers exist in its relations to the States and the peoples of the States. Exercising all its powers, incidental and implied, it is not, in its efforts at self-preservation, to acquire any new power, or to subvert any of the powers of the States, or the liberties of the people as citizens of the States.

Its right of self-preservation is to keep itself as it is, not only in reference to its own existence and power, but in reference also to the existence and powers of the States, and the liberties of the peoples of the States.

This right of self-preservation, therefore, does not avail anything towards supporting the argument that the nation has a right to treat the "States lately in rebellion" as conquered States, or to deny them a representation in Congress, because of the treason committed by the citizens of a State.

A few words further upon "reconstruction," which, as the result of all these various theories of the loss of State rights, it is so violently insisted, must take place before the disorganized States can be represented in Congress, and which it is also insisted, is within the power of Congress alone.

The rebellion was of such extent, that the contest was *not* between the government on one side, and a handful of insurgents on the other, of such limited numbers that only a small exertion of the military power was required to suppress it. It involved, to a greater or less extent, nearly all the people of eleven of the States. The State governments were in the hands of the rebels, who professed to exercise the powers of those governments as if they were legitimately in their possession, and to do this in opposition to, and in subversion of, the authority of the United States. In whatever light this may be viewed, so far as the States themselves were concerned, and in relation to their local affairs, it was, as to the United States, a usurpation of the State authority, for the purposes of treason. The United States could not regard such an administration of the State governments as lawful. As to that government, it was an overturning of the lawful administration of the State governments, and the substitution of an unlawful one as if it were a lawful one, and this was usurpation. By this usurpation the action of the State governments was brought in conflict with the government of the United States, but the States themselves were not thereby destroyed. There was no attempt on the part of the rebels to change their ordinances, or to subvert their constitutions. And if there had been such an attempt, it would not have availed anything against the United States government, which remained with all its powers, legislative, executive, and judicial, unimpaired (notwithstanding their exercise was obstructed) within those States.

The rebels also organized a confederate government, embracing those States, with powers of a national character, like unto those of the United States. This was a new creation, unlawful, treasonable, void, as against the United States.

The termination of the war, by the surrender and disbanding of the forces organized by this confederate government, terminated at the same time the existence of the confederate government, and it terminated, also, the administration of the powers of the State governments in hostility to the United States. But it did not terminate the existence of the several States. It terminated what was unlawful. It did not subvert what was lawful. The war was prosecuted for the purpose of subverting the confederacy and overcoming the rebellion; but was not, and could not have been, prosecuted for the purpose of overthrowing the States, consistently with the obligations of the United States, particularly the obligation to guarantee to them a republican form of government, — an obligation which the United States owed, not only to those States whose people were in rebellion, but to all the States, — to New Hampshire as well as to South Carolina. The Northern States had an equal interest in the due performance of this duty by the United States with the Southern States. All the Northern States had an interest in the preservation of the Southern States, as members of the Union. An interest which the United States government had no right to overrule or disregard. Any attempt on the part of the United States to prosecute the war for the purpose of subverting or extinguishing the existence of those eleven States whose people were in rebellion, or any one of them, would have been revolutionary. And so any attempt by means of the war to subvert the rights of those States, as States, must be of the same character.

The States could not constitutionally secede from their place in the Union. It is equally true that the United States could not constitutionally turn them out.

The conclusion then is irresistible, to any one who reasons upon legal, and not upon revolutionary principles, not only that all which was necessary to be done, but all which could constitutionally be done, on the close of the war, was to reorganize the governments of those States. Until this could be done, the military possession of the territory which had been acquired by the success of the war could be continued for the purpose of preserving the peace, and for the purpose of such an administration of justice as the military power might properly interpose in the mean time, limited by the ordinary exercise of military power in the suppression of a rebellion.

But how was this reorganization to be effected?

If there had been any provision of the Constitution of the United States, by which on the disorganization of a State government, by the loss of the officers authorized to administer its affairs, the President, or Congress, or the Secretary of State, or any other official, was authorized to issue a proclamation for primary meetings, to be held under the Constitution and laws of such State, for the election of the officers necessary to organize the State government, and put it again into operation; it would only have been necessary that the party thus designated should have issued the proclamation, accordingly, and then the people of the State, assembling and acting in accordance with it, the reorganization would have been effected in a regular manner. But there was no provision of the kind.

If there had been a provision in the constitutions of the several disorganized States, by which such a proclamation could be issued by any officer still holding office, or the president or librarian of some college, or the clerk or sexton of some regularly organized society, then the reorganization might have been had in the mode thus prescribed in the several States. But there was no such provision anywhere.

No such case had been contemplated, and all provision for such an occurrence had been omitted.

It is clear enough that the omission of such a provision, because it did not enter into the imagination of any one that it could, if inserted, be of any possible use, did not change the nature of the case, so far as the continued existence of the several States was concerned. The States were there with their powers and rights as before the war. The question was how to bring those powers into action again. Evidently there must be an assumption of authority somewhere to provide for taking the first step for an election of State officers. Who should assume it?

As there was no State legislature to act, and as the act to be done was in its nature executive and not legislative, — an order or notice, by an assumption of power, for the purpose, — Congress, which is not the depositary of executive power, was not the proper party to interfere. On the other hand, the circumstances indicated clearly that the President was the party who should take this first step. There was no State officer who could with propriety make such an assumption.

By the Constitution of the United States, the President is commander of the army and navy, and the army and navy, under the orders of the President, were in possession and authority, so far as any authority could be exercised.

There was to be a withdrawal of these forces, and the substitution of a civil rule and authority. In the absence of any provision for the purpose, who so proper to regulate the transition from one to the other, as the officer who held the right and power to terminate the military occupation, and who ought not to terminate it until some provision was made for the substitution of civil authority?

In assuming to provide for this transition from military government to a reorganization of the State governments, the President, instead of issuing a proclamation directly calling upon the people to assemble and choose officers, very judiciously interposed the appointment of provisional governors, and intrusted to them the duty, if it may be so termed, of calling the primary meetings, and in that manner made the organization, in appearance, more nearly like an act of the State, which it should have been, had it been a possibility.

He interposed a requirement that the constitutions of the several States should be amended so as to abolish slavery, and that the amendment of the Constitution of the United States for that purpose should be adopted, so as to secure the abolition against any further action of the State.

It may be admitted that there was no constitutional authority for this, and as it was a requirement that the people of those States should surrender what had been admitted to be a political right of those States, its character was essentially different from that of any act intended merely to effect the reorganization of the States. In other words it was usurpation, and revolutionary.

In this view, however, it was not without some palliation.

The existence of slavery had been for a long time the subject of a bitter controversy between the different sections, which had culminated in the attempt to dissolve the Union by force. Whatever other causes existed behind this, the pretext for rebellion was found here.

After a vast sacrifice of life, and an enormous expenditure of money, on the part of the Northern States, in the suppression of the attempt at revolution on the part of the Southern people, it was but natural, when the rebellion was suppressed, that the successful party should insist upon the removal of the root of bitterness which had been made the means of such a disastrous conflict between the two sections, in order to prevent further controversies of a like character in the future; even if there was no constitutional warrant for the abolition of slavery except by the States where it existed, and the action therefore revolutionary. The United States had been obliged to resort to the law of force to preserve the Union, and it was apparent that the same law of force which had been put in operation by the rebels, could on the termination of the conflict be made available to accomplish the abolition. Those who set the machinery in motion could not reasonably object. As an act of revolution, I am inclined to excuse and even justify a requirement on the part of the people of the Northern States that slavery should be abolished. At the same time I regret that there were no sufficient guards provided to make the abolition a blessing instead of a curse to vast numbers of those who were thus suddenly set free. And I condemn, unreservedly, the attempt to shield this act under any pretence of an authority, under the Constitution, to abolish slavery, or to require it to be done, because that is perverting the Constitution, and in evil example hereafter.

In consequence of this action of the President, meetings were called in the several States, delegates elected, conventions assembled, constitutions amended, officers of the State governments elected, and the military occupation was withdrawn, except for certain limited purposes, such as the protection of the freedmen in the just possession of the rights which they had acquired by the emancipation. Reorganization was thus effected. This was "reconstruction" in one, and the only legitimate sense of the term in that connection. If the States were in the Union all the time, because they could not secede and go out from it, this reorganization, under the action of the President, was all the reconstruction which was necessary to enable them to act again in their proper sphere within the Union.

But this was not reconstruction in the sense of those who have been clamorous for reconstruction. They were seeking to accomplish something beyond the reorganization of the States, and the restoration of their relations to the Union by means of such reorganization. They were seeking to force upon those States a radical change of their institutions, not in relation to the alleged cause of the war only, but in relation to certain rights of their citizens, which in all the other States are, and have been, from the foundation of the government, acted on as matters properly within the control of the States, — in relation to matters which, even at the present day, are not only determined by the Northern States according to their will and pleasure, but by rules directly the reverse of those which are sought to be enforced against the Southern States, — matters respecting which until recently no one ventured to suggest a doubt of the right of each State to adopt its own measures, — matters over which the government of the United States has no control, except by usurpation.

These new measures of reconstruction are urged under the plausible but hollow pretence of protection to the freedman in the rights acquired by his emancipation; but the truth is, that they have regard mainly to the retention of political power in the party now in possession of it.

Singular as it may seem, it nevertheless appears as if those who so vigorously urged immediate unconditional emancipation did not, until after the constitutional amendment providing for emancipation was before the people, awake to the realization of the fact, that the emancipation would enlarge, to a very great extent, the representation of the Southern States in Congress, under the existing law of apportionment, while the right of suffrage, under the existing State laws, would remain in the same class of persons who had previously exercised that right; for if that result had been then seen by them, it would have been the part of wisdom to have provided a new rule of apportionment by the new amendment to the Constitution. Or shall we suppose, that seeing this effect of the emancipation, under the existing laws, it was thought that the purposes of the party might be best subserved by revolutionary measures, denying to the Southern States any representation, or only such as the party pleased to accord to them, from time to time, when in this or that locality men were elected who would train faithfully in the congressional party ranks, and, irrespective of the requirements of the Constitution and laws, do the bidding of the leaders of the party.

For the purpose of securing the party ascendency, the State governments, as organized by the direction of the President, in their connection with the Union, have been substantially overthrown again by congressional action, — about as effectually subverted by Congress as they were by the rebellion, — and the States themselves, in relation to their internal affairs, placed in a much worse state of disorganization.

I have followed and exposed the doctrines of this class of constitutional politicians, until the work has become burdensome. It seems as if there was no end to their hollow pretences. Each demagogue in Congress strives to invent some new theory, and if unable to do that, then to attach an amendment, or improvement in sophistry upon the vicious constitutional notions of some one else who has preceded him. The boldest of all these unconstitutional dogmas, is, perhaps, an allegation that the Southern States may be reconstructed under the "war power," because the war is not ended.

In connection with other efforts by Congress to change the constitutional relations of the United States, and of the several

States, the Fourteenth Amendment deserves some consideration, as a part of the measures of reconstruction.

The words "the Congress" and "Congress," are used indiscriminately in the Constitution in two different senses. When used in reference to the legislative authority of the United States, these terms include the President also, so far as his power of approval or veto is involved in the legislation. Thus the Constitution provides that "the Congress shall have power to lay and collect taxes, duties, imposts, and excises;" "to regulate commerce with foreign nations;" "the Congress may at any time, by law, make or alter" "regulations respecting the election of senators and representatives," &c.; "No State shall, without the consent of the Congress, lay any imposts, or duties on imports or exports, except what may be absolutely necessary for executing its inspection laws," &c.; "and all such laws shall be subject to the revision and control of the Congress. No State shall, without the consent of Congress, lay any duty of tonnage," &c.

The action of "the Congress" in cases of this character is legislative, appropriately manifested through some bill or resolution; and the Constitution provides that "every bill which shall have passed the House of Representatives and the Senate shall be presented to the President" for his approval, and "every order, resolution, or vote, to which the concurrence of the Senate and House of Representatives may be necessary (except on a question of adjournment), shall be presented" in like manner.

This is the general use of the terms. But when the Constitution provides that "all legislative powers herein granted shall be vested in a Congress of the United States, which shall consist of a Senate and House of Representatives," and when it provides further that the President "shall from time to time give to the Congress information of the state of the Union," it is clear that only the two Houses are intended.

And this is perhaps true of the use of the term "Congress," when the Constitution speaks of "the first meeting of the Congress," although this phraseology might be construed to include the President also, in the same manner that he is included in relation to the passage of laws, if it were of any importance that it should bear that construction.

The fifth article of the Constitution provides that "the Congress, whenever two thirds of both Houses shall deem it necessary, shall propose amendments to this Constitution, or, on the application of the legislatures of two thirds of the several States, shall call a convention for proposing amendments, which, in either case, shall be valid, to all intents and purposes, as part of this Constitution, when ratified by the legislatures of three fourths of the several States, or by conventions in three fourths thereof, as the one or the other mode of ratification may be proposed by the Congress," &c.

"The Congress" "shall propose,"—"may be proposed by the Congress"! The act through and by which this proposition is to be made, takes, of course, the shape of a "bill," or "order, resolution, or vote," and it is an act to which the concurrence of the Senate and House is necessary. That is clear. Is the assent or approval of the President necessary in order that it should be a proposition by the Congress?—as his approval is necessary in order that other things should be laws enacted by the Congress, unless the two Houses pass the bill, order, or resolution, by a two thirds vote.

At the session of Congress in June, 1866, four propositions, diverse in their character and objects, were included in a single article, by the two Houses of Congress, and sent out as a proposed amendment to the Constitution.

The first declares that all persons born or naturalized in the United States, and subject to the jurisdiction thereof, are citizens of the United States, and of the State where they reside; and it forbids any State to make a law which shall abridge the privileges of citizens of the United States, or to deprive any person of life, liberty, or property, without due process of law; or to deny to any person within its jurisdiction the equal protection of the law.[1]

The second has regard to the apportionment of representatives, and the basis of representation, making it to depend in some measure upon a denial or abridgment by a State of a right of its male citizens to vote in certain State elections.

The third disables any person who has taken an oath to support the Constitution of the United States, and afterwards has en-

1 May a State admit any other persons as citizens? Does "due process of law" include trial by jury?

gaged in insurrection or rebellion, from being representative or senator in Congress, elector of President or Vice-President, and from holding any office, civil or military, under the United States or any State. But Congress may, by a vote of two thirds, remove the disability.

The fourth provides that the public debt of the United States, authorized by law, shall not be questioned. But neither the United States, nor any State, shall assume or pay any debt incurred in aid of insurrection or rebellion, or any compensation for loss of slaves; but all such debts, obligations, and claims, shall be void.

It is readily seen that here are four amendments. But there is but one vote to be taken on them.

There has been no approval by the President, nor any presentment for approval; but the propositions have been sent to the several States, the Southern States as well as others, for their ratification.

It is evident that the two Houses intended that they should be sent to "the States lately in rebellion" (as the phrase is) as well as other States.

If amendments "proposed by the Congress" require the approval of the President, these propositions have not been proposed for ratification in a constitutional mode, and the whole proceeding is nugatory, at least as regards States not ratifying.

It may be urged that the term "the Congress" in this connection, means the two Houses; and that notwithstanding the proposal is to be by bill, order, resolution, or vote, the approval of the President is not necessary, because this is not a matter of legislation, but a special power, and there is no provision for passing such a proposition by the two Houses in case the President should withhold his assent, two thirds of both Houses being required in the first instance, and that it could not have been intended that the proposing of amendments should be at the pleasure of the President.

It is quite clear that the power vested in the Congress by the fifth article is not an ordinary legislative power.

It is a special power. We will assume that a proposition for amendment has not the character of a legislative act, and that the assent of the President is not required.

As the power, then, is not one of ordinary legislation, it has no claim to be governed or construed by the rules which govern ordinary legislation.

As it is a special power, it must be construed and exercised with reference to its object, and its operation in relation to the several States to which propositions for amendments may be made.

Now, it can hardly need an argument to show that the spirit, intention, purpose, and object of this provision require that "the Congress," if the two Houses propose more than one amendment, shall propose each amendment as a separate and distinct proposition, so that no proposed amendment shall embrace two or more propositions, distinct and diverse in their general character.

The reason for such a construction is obvious. If Congress may couple four dissimilar amendments together, this action may be the means of depriving the States of constitutional amendments, which three fourths of the States desire to adopt, but which they refuse because coupled with others which they disapprove; or of imposing upon them the necessity of adopting amendments which they, in fact, disapprove, but which they vote to adopt rather than lose others in which they have a great and controlling interest. And if it may operate in this way upon the majority of the States, its operation may be much more objectionable upon the minority, which in this way may, in other cases, have imposed upon them amendments against which they have voted, none of which would have obtained a constitutional majority if they had been proposed separately.

It is no answer to this to say that the same thing may occur in the adoption of an entire constitution, which must be adopted entirely or not at all. An entire constitution is almost entirely made up of several parts fitted and joined together, and in relation to most of these parts they should stand or fall together, being dependent upon each other. It is not so with proposed congressional amendments. The body of the work has already been adopted. The amendments are adjuncts to it.

Moreover, the authority of Congress is not to propose an entire constitution, but to propose amendments to the existing Constitution.

Nor can any support of such a course of coupling dissimilar

amendments, be derived from the fact that legislative bodies, and especially Congress, are in their ordinary legislation in the habit of coupling diverse propositions in what is sometimes called an " omnibus bill," which is objectionable in itself. That cannot be used as a precedent in proposing constitutional amendments, which, we have admitted, is not an act of ordinary legislation, nor legislative in its character, but one done under a special power.

Furthermore: the proposal of an article by which the States must adopt all or none of several distinct amendments of different natures, and having different objects, while it is contrary to sound principle, has not only no warrant in the language of the Constitution, but has no support in any practice under it. The first and fifth of the amendments which have been adopted might seem at first sight to countenance such a procedure. But it does not require a critical inspection to perceive that each is made an entire thing consisting of several particulars. The first is a prohibition upon Congress to *interfere with the liberty of the citizen* by an establishment of religion, or by prohibiting the free exercise of it, or by abridging the freedom of speech, or the press, or the right of the people peaceably to assemble and petition for a redress of grievances. The fifth is a provision *for the security of liberty and property*, consisting of several particulars; namely, "No person shall be held to answer for a capital, or otherwise infamous crime, unless on a presentment or indictment by a grand jury, except in cases arising in the land or naval forces, or in the militia when in actual service in time of war or public danger; nor shall any person be subject for the same offence to be twice put in jeopardy of life or limb; nor shall he be compelled in any criminal case to be a witness against himself, nor be deprived of life, liberty, or property, without due process of law; nor shall private property be taken for public use, without just compensation."

Another, and a very grave objection to this article of amendment is, that the first and second propositions tend to change the fundamental relations of the United States, and the several States, by an interference with the internal concerns of the States, certainly not contemplated in the original Constitution. How far may such a process of amendment be carried, under the congressional power to propose amendments, to be adopted by three fourths of the people, or of the *legislatures* of the States?

If the people of the whole country had been a nation, from the Declaration of Independence, with power to adopt a Constitution for the whole country, without regard to that much abused thing called State rights (and such a power would have existed on that state of facts), and if the Constitution had been so adopted, — then Congress, having general legislative power, might, notwithstanding the special provision of the Constitution respecting amendments to be proposed to the States, pass an act to ascertain the will of the people in regard to a convention for the purpose of amending the Constitution, and the convention if called, might put the Constitution into a new draft, and by a major vote of the whole people State rights might be obliterated.

But Congress, — under the Constitution, as it exists, adopted not by any nation, but by the peoples of the several States, who surrendered some of the powers of the States, and granted limited powers to the United States, among them this power to propose amendments, — has no power to call such a convention, or to provide for any vote of the whole people upon the subject. Amendments are to be made only in the mode prescribed.

It will hardly be contended, even by the advocates of the ante-national theory, that Congress, under the special power to propose amendments, can send forth one for adoption by the legislatures, or even by the people, of three fourths of the States, which shall operate to extinguish the authority of the States, and turn them into counties of the United States. Why not? Because Congress is not authorized to propose, as *amendments*, provisions which will subvert the Constitution, and the States which gave it existence. That would not be an *amendment* of the Constitution, but the *destruction* of it. How far then, may the process of amendment be carried to the prejudice of the fundamental principles which governed the relation of the United States to the several States on its original adoption, as shown by the instrument itself? I may not answer this question at the present time, but I commend it to your careful consideration.

It is worthy of remark here that this article is proposed to "the States lately in rebellion." It is transmitted to State authorities under the organization which has been had through the measures of the President. It is true that it is thus transmitted to those States by the Department of State; but the article appears to have been passed by the two Houses of Congress with the intention that it should thus be transmitted to those States, for consideration by these very State legislatures. It was intended to affect them more particularly than any other States, and the adoption of it by them was the very thing which was intended to be compelled by the refusal to admit their senators and representatives to seats in Congress.

Not only so, but the former amendment abolishing slavery was in like manner transmitted to those States, to be acted on by the legislatures under that reorganization through the action of the President, and was adopted by them, and the act of adoption received as effectual for the amendment of the Constitution.

Now these facts prove, conclusively, not only that the reorganization through the measures inaugurated by the President was rightful, enabling the people once more to proceed with their local elections, and thus to organize a legitimate legislature not only for local and State purposes, but also for all purposes connected with its existence as a State in the Union.

And if the people could thus elect a legislature which could receive and adopt an amendment to the Constitution, that legislature might well elect senators, and the people who constituted it could elect representatives in Congress.

A constitutional amendment can only be proposed for adoption to a State in the Union. The propositions by Congress, admit that they are in the Union. A denial after this, that these States are in the Union, by any person who assumes to reason upon the subject, fairly exposes such person to the suspicion of some little deficiency in the region of the cerebral organs, or of such an absorbing devotion to party as obscures any ordinary perception of an unwelcome political truth.

LECTURE III.

THE THREE DANGERS OF THE REPUBLIC.

[Law School of Harvard College, January, 1868. Dartmouth College, April, 1869.]

Gentlemen of the Law School: —

SOME brief recognition of that portion of the political excitements which have an immediate connection with the laws of the country, and which must exert an immense force, either for good or for evil, upon the institutions of government under which we live, seems to be not only appropriate, but perhaps to be demanded of an educational institution designed to prepare young men to take an active part in the administration of justice. Such men necessarily exercise a great influence upon the destinies of the country. If you may not control the course of current events, you may and must do much either in support of, or in opposition to, the measures which shape the future of the Republic.

Within the present term my attention was accidentally attracted to a leading editorial in the New York Evening Post, entitled, "Some Cheering Signs," in which three signs of encouragement were enumerated and discussed. The first two related to the President's discretion, and to changes in the Cabinet, and were of no material consequence. But the third was of a wider significance, containing a long extract from the New York World, upon which much commendation was bestowed. The mere fact that those two papers should agree upon any political subject, naturally created some surprise, which was not lessened upon an examination of the extract, which was introduced by the "Post" in this wise: —

"In the third place, the democratic party, which conceives itself on the eve of a splendid national triumph — whether rightly or wrongly does not concern us here — in considering how it shall consolidate success, secure the future, and discharge the high responsibilities implied in success, seems disposed to reconsider its position and essentially recast its plans of action. In the speeches made the other night by Messrs. Hoffman and Tilden, but particularly in an article in the 'World' of this morning — an article of great penetration, thoughtfulness, and candor, which we have read with unaffected pleasure — we discover evidences of forecast, and of a sense of duty to the country, which are encouraging. Listen to these words, evidently sincere and well considered."

Then follows the extract from the "World": —

"The democratic party must be wise enough to recognize the moulding influence of great events on public opinion, and the permanence of some of their consequences. Even in the most tranquil times, society and public opinion are in a state of constant, and in a new country like this, of rapid growth. In a period of convulsive turbulence and upheaving, opinion advances with an accelerated velocity. It is not possible that the mighty struggles of the last six years should not leave a deep imprint on succeeding times. The future of this country is not to depend on the opinions of men who were over forty when the war broke out, but on the opinions of those who were under thirty. Though built after the same plan, our older men will say, like those of Israel, that the second temple is not like the first. We must nevertheless recognize facts. *It is a fact that all the flower of our young men were engaged in, and educated by, the war. All the youthful vigor, daring, enterprise, love of adventure, thirst for honor, pride of country, marched with our armies. In the army they lived a deeper life than falls to the lot of ordinary sluggish generations. Their whole manhood was a hundred times put to the proof; the experience of four years was more than the common experience of a life.* And it came at an age when the character is yet pliant and yielding; when opinions are either not formed, or have not settled into dogmatic stiffness. The mould was applied while the clay was yet soft, and it will continue to bear the impress. There is an ineffaceable difference between the generation of men that is going out and the younger generation that is coming in; and no party which ignores this difference will be in sufficient sympathy with the rising future to guide its politics. Our elderly men, whose habits of thought became fixed before the war, will be every year deserting, in obedience to a summons they cannot resist. As between the old epoch and the new, they will be a constantly dwindling minority; but as between the living and the dead, they are 'passing over to the majority.' Their indurated habits of thought will pass with them, and the country will be ruled by the generation whose character was shaped in these later stirring times.

"The democratic party, in its brightest and palmiest days, was preëminently the party of progress. In spite of the croakings and forebodings of its opponents, it extended the suffrage to white citizens till suffrage became universal; it abolished imprisonment for debt; removed the property qualification for office; made the State judiciary elective; brought new territory into the Union until its original area was quadrupled; made vigorous war upon the protective system, although many of its early leaders had supported it; and until the slavery question became predominant, its favorite employment was to supply fresh fuel to the engine rather than to put on the brakes. *In complaisance to its southern wing it made mistakes on the slavery question and lost the advantage of leadership. In its attempts to prevent opinion advancing too fast it fell behind; and there could not be a more fatal blunder, at present, than an attempt to carry the public opinion of the country back* to the point where it stood when, to save the train from destruction in moving down a declivity, the democratic party went from the engine to the brakes."

Upon which the "Post" thus comments: —

"What does all that mean? Why, that copperheadism, which has made the democratic party odious, must be thrown overboard; that a dead and stagnant conservatism is to be abandoned; that the old pro-slavery affinities, which have been a clog and a mistake, must be cut loose, and that the life and vigor of the young men of the nation, of the men who fought the battles of the Union, must be taken as the inspiration and guide of policy. We congratulate the World on the gracefulness with which it lets itself down, or, more properly, on the manliness with which it raises itself up to the position which the Evening Post long since predicted it must occupy if it and its party wish to place themselves on a level with the real democratic sentiment of the nation."

There is certainly a significance in this. These papers claim to be among the leading journals of the country. And such positive assertions respecting the future of the democratic party, by the leading conservative paper of that party, — assertions which cause such jubilation in the radical organ of the other wing, — so radical that it has differed in nothing from the most superlatively radical of the republican press, except in the name, — must have a meaning respecting the course and policy of the country, of a very important character.

It is true, that the matter is vague enough in some of its particulars. But in others it is clear.

There is, or is to be, a new epoch. The future of the country is not to depend on the opinions of men who were over forty when the war broke out. The opinions of men *under thirty* are to be the ruling opinions. They were educated by the war, and have lived a *deeper life* than falls to the lot of ordinary sluggish generations. In the army, within the period of four years, they have had more than the common experience of a life. Their characters were then pliant and yielding. The mould was applied while the clay was soft, and the impress exhibits an *ineffaceable difference* between the incoming and outgoing generation, which last is to become a constantly dwindling minority among the living, but with the encouragement that its members may, by dying, attain the acme of a politician's aspirations, that is, pass into the *majority*. "Their indurated habits of thought," it is stated, "will pass with them," which is, I suppose, the democratic mode of expressing the scriptural benediction, "their works do follow them." The country is to to be ruled by the "generation whose character was shaped in these later times."

So far, so clear. Curiosity might inquire whether persons over *forty*, who administer a sufficient amount of flattery to the men under *thirty*, who have acquired such a large experience in the science of government by serving four years in the army, are not expecting to share in the offices, and whether those men under thirty, whose characters have received the mould, and will continue to bear the indelible impress (and who of course must have *their* indurated habits of thought by the time they are forty), are, in the same remorseless way, to be consigned over to that majority which never troubles the active politician, giving way to another set under thirty, who, in order to possess equal qualifications, must be educated in another war, in which they can obtain the experience of a long life in four years? But I am not curious on these subjects.

You will note that all this is said of those portions of the incoming generation which participated in the active service of the war, *not in relation to the acquisition of vigorous constitutions, readiness of action, strong will, and manliness of character, but in regard to the experience and qualifications which will enable them to govern the country, to mould anew its institutions, to direct its policy, and to shape its destiny.*

There is to be a second temple, which our older men will say is not like the first. The worship, of course, is to be adapted to the new order of things, and I have anxiously explored the text, and the commentary, to ascertain, if possible, wherein the temple and the worship are to differ from those of the fathers.

The oracle of the text, and the oracle of the commentary are to some extent uncertain, but by a careful study we gain some insight into our future.

The democratic party, which was preëminently the party of progress, is to be so again. Copperheadism (the true signification and meaning of which term, in its most usual application to persons at the North, is, *ardent disinterested patriotism, and sincere love of the country and its political institutions*,) is to be thrown overboard; the conservatism which fears untried experiments upon the institutions founded by the fathers, is to be abandoned; the wisdom of the past is to be ignored and disregarded; the life and vigor of the young men who fought the battles of the Union are to be the inspiration and guide of its policy.

The talk about cutting loose from the old pro-slavery affinities is mere clap-trap, unless it means that we are to have no consideration for the people of the Southern States; for slavery having been abolished by an amendment of the Constitution, there can be no pro-slavery affinities to cut loose from, and there can be no blunder, fatal or otherwise, of returning to a support of slavery.

But the democratic party is not to attempt to carry the public opinion of the country back to the constitutional principles which were admitted and acknowledged before the war, — it is not to commit the fatal blunder of putting on the brakes, when the train is running down a declivity, even to save it from destruction, — but it is to follow up its favorite employment of supplying fresh fuel to the engine, and to hasten with increased velocity on the downward grade. In other words, it is to enter into a lively competition with the radical wing of the republican party, in the hope of once more obtaining the Presidency and Treasurership of the company, and the power of appointing the engineers, conductors, ticket sellers, switchmen, lamplighters, &c.

Well, the track of a nation, like that of a railroad, is not a straight, level, smooth line for any great distance. It has its deep cuts and embankments to run through and over, its curves and its sidings, its defective rails, and its occasional obstructions. Upon the principle suggested, the trackmen and the switchmen should cast away their old conservatism, as well as the engineers. The conductors must busy themselves exclusively in collecting and pocketing the fares, — and the national train must rush down the declivity at a rate of speed never before conceived of in the progress of nations.

If a bent axle causes an Angola disaster, by which a train is thrown down an embankment and the imprisoned passengers burned alive, what must be the terrible catastrophe and ruin, the horrible torture of those who are crushed to death under the wreck of the nation, and what the lamentations and wailings of the survivors, which must inevitably follow a national progress like this!

But, dropping the very significant metaphor in which these advocates of progress have seen fit to clothe their conceptions of the glorious future, to which they are to add their contributions, — let us inquire in plain prose, what is to be done, in fact, by this party of progress.

We are left to learn this in a great measure by what it is said has been done by the democratic party heretofore. What it has done, it may continue to do, so long as there is room for its enterprise. We are told that it extended the suffrage to white citizens until it became universal. This is certainly a strange declaration, in the face of the fact that all the young men who in the army led that *deeper life, four years of which better qualifies a man to guide its politics, than the common experience of a whole life passed elsewhere*, have not yet a constitutional right of suffrage, unless they have attained the age of twenty-one years. If suffrage is to be made universal, there is much to be done here.

Next it is said that the democratic party abolished imprisonment for debt. That, certainly, is not to be done over again. The only progress to be made in this line is to abolish imprisonment for non-payment of damages for wrongs committed (if it has not already extended to that), which would make no very marked change in the life of the nation; and to abolish it, likewise, as a punishment for crimes committed, which certainly would be progress in some direction. The property qualification for office having been removed, no progress seems necessary in that direction, except to secure the offices.

An elective judiciary! Progress may still be made there by electing the judges annually, by a popular vote. But that matter comes home so nearly to men's business, that even those who have lived the "deeper life" will hardly trifle much with it. An elective judiciary has been generally found to be an error, except in Vermont, where the judges are elected annually by the legislature, and where they have a practical remedy for a bad constitution, by reëlecting their judges, as a general rule, so long as they are qualified.

Bringing new territory into the Union! Here is an ample field for a very mischievous progress, — sure, if pursued, to be attended with its legitimate consequences.

Vigorous war upon the protective system! Until the national debt is either paid or repudiated, this cannot well be a war to the knife. Progress here must be very tortoise-footed.

This is the summary given of the progress heretofore made by the democratic party. What new worlds there are for it to conquer, hereafter, does not appear.

I have taken this text and commentary as an exponent of the spirit of radicalism, not merely on account of the importance of the sources from which they emanate, but because they are in accordance with many kindred utterances, and indicate, in a general way, the platform on which the radical spirit of progress seeks to retain its power; and the purpose which it designs to accomplish.

Utterances like these, through the press, in the halls of Congress, in conventions, and wherever else mere politicians make themselves heard, may serve to show us *three*, — I think I may say — *the three great* dangers of the Republic, two of them shadowed forth in some of the objects which are apparently to be attained, — the third, being the moving cause which produces all this agitation about progress, by the parties who for selfish purposes seek to excite a self-sufficiency in the younger generation, and to lead them to despise the indurated conservatism of any one over forty years of age.

The dangers to which I allude, are —

1. An undue extension of territory.

2d. An undue extension of the right of suffrage, — and

3d. An undue desire for office, — a hankering after place and power, not to serve one's country, but for the promotion of selfish purposes, — this last being the greatest danger of all.

It is something more than three quarters of a century, since the formation of the government of the United States; and these three quarters of a century may serve very nearly as three epochs in its history.

It was formed by the peoples of the several States, as a substitute for the Confederacy, to which they had surrendered a very limited portion of the sovereignty of their several States, and by a surrender of a further portion of that sovereignty for the purpose of endowing it with sufficient power to accomplish the purposes of its formation. The peoples of the several States were very tenacious of their rights under the State governments, — in many instances surrendered them with extreme reluctance, and with great fear that the powers granted would be used or abused, to the subversion of the rights of the States and of the people. And by amendments to the original constitution, adopted immediately after the government was organized and which it was understood would be adopted when the Constitution was ratified, they placed, as they fondly supposed, such express limitations upon its power, that the sovereignty of the States and the liberties of the people were reasonably secured.

Still its operation was watched with no little jealousy.

Notwithstanding the men to whom its administration was committed in the first instance were of eminent ability, actuated by the purest patriotism, and who exercised their untried powers with the greatest caution, questions of construction in regard to different clauses of the Constitution necessarily arose from the outset; and a great question respecting the final arbiter for the determination of such disputed questions, — or according to the phrase of the day, the question, what was the remedy for the abuse of its powers, — which has since led to attempts at nullification, and finally furnished the foundation for the rebellion of 1861, — was the subject of virulent controversy, upon which parties divided within the first ten years of the existence of the government.

The territory of the United States was then limited, on the South by the Floridas, on the West by the Mississippi, (the western bank of which was in the possession of Spain), and by the territorial possessions of Great Britain on the North; and within these limits there was vacant space enough, so far to satisfy the people of that day, that no provision was inserted in the Constitution having in view the acquisition of further territory, — although, through the power to make war, the power to form treaties, and to make regulations of commerce, acquisition of territory undoubtedly might be made.

It must have been evident that some provision would eventually become necessary for the commerce of the Mississippi, but no one was bold enough to propose the insertion into the Constitution of a clause directly authorizing the acquisition of additional territory for that purpose.

During the first period of twenty-five years, Louisiana was acquired, as a necessity, to secure a post at the outlet of the Mississippi river, but under a stormy opposition, so strong on the part of a distinguished representative from Massachusetts that he declared it as his deliberate opinion that if the purchase was consummated the bonds of the Union would be virtually dissolved, that the States which composed it would be free from their moral obligations, and that as it would be the right of all, so it would be the duty of some, to prepare definitely for a separation, " amicably if they can, violently if they must."

Here is the assertion of right of secession or of a right of revolution, for an alleged usurpation of power by the General Government, in the extension of territory, comprised within the limits of a nutshell, and coming from a representative of Massachusetts without rebuke from his constituents.

The second period was one of comparative quiet, and of general prosperity. It seemed as if the experiment was no longer problematical.

But in this period Florida was purchased, to give greater facilities for navigation upon the Gulf. " The extension of the area of freedom " had lost some of its terrors.

The third period was one of political storm and tempest, embracing near its commencement the annexation of Texas, and the acquisition of California, — and ending in the rebellion of 1861, which, we are all well advised, shook the Union to its foundations, and for a long time gravely threatened its disruption.

After all that has been said of slavery, as the cause of the war, and important as was the part which that institution had in producing it, — and after making all allowance for conflicting industrial interests as furnishing the primal reason for it, — we may, I think, safely conclude, that but for acquisition of Louisiana and Florida, and perhaps of Texas also, that war would never have had an existence.

I shall not detain you by arguing this matter in detail, at this time. I think a moment's reflection will convince you, that confined within the original limits, or, with the addition of a small territory at the mouth of the Mississippi, the people of the Southern States could never have so overestimated their strength, as to enter into a contest with the rest of the Union.

The acquisition of California has, thus far, given strength to the Union instead of subjecting it to peril. Whether the end of the fourth epoch may find the same state of things, is known only to Omniscience.

But we must note the facts, that the territory west of the Rocky mountains is fast filling with a busy, enterprising population, — that there is territory there sufficient for an empire,— that the direct means of intercourse, even after the Pacific railroad shall have connected the two sections, will be very limited, — and that the difficulties of contending with a formidable rebellion there would be almost insuperable.

Alaska is, of itself, comparatively unimportant, in reference to this question. It is not likely of its own weight to sever itself from its connection with us, if that be consummated. But it may furnish a convenient appendage to California and Oregon, whenever the people of those States throw off their allegiance.

It seems that the warnings of history, and of our own experience, are to be lost to us.

Our plans of aggrandizement, through an extension of our territory, are apparently to have no limit.

We are to "take up the isles as a very little thing." And to annex South America, if not by a single operation, at least by large sections.

How far are we to extend in that direction without disunion?

The Southern States, although wasted and impoverished by the war, are once more to become prosperous, — more so than ever before. Even the members of the party of progress are desirous of that, when they shall have fitted those States for political freedom, by such a proper adjustment of the suffrage as will secure to that party the offices and emoluments.

Will it not be well for us to recollect, that there was *another army*, in which the young men also lived that *deeper life*, and acquired the experience of the same four years; that we are teaching them to continue our enemies, instead of endeavoring to make them our friends, — that if they complained of wrongs before the war, they are not likely to consider them redressed by the peace, still less by the measures of reconstruction since the peace, — that this hostility has been already sufficiently fostered by those measures, to be transmitted by inheritance, even unto the third and fourth generations, — and finally that every acquisition of territory on their Southern borders, is but adding strength to the next rebellion, for which we are daily educating them or their descendants, through the hatred which we teach them.

I turn next to the second of the dangers which I have enumerated: —

The undue extension of the right of suffrage.

Suffrage, in a republic, is a personal power of government, — the primary power. The people by their votes elect persons to represent them in making the laws, because it is impracticable that this power, the most important of all, lying at the foundation of government, can be exercised directly by the great body of the people.

In the exercise of this power, each one does, or may do, something towards the government of all the other members of the community. His vote may determine who shall be the successful candidate; and the successful candidate, in the exercise of his office, may determine the passage of laws which affect the property, and persons, even the life, of other members of the community.

The proposition, therefore, that there is a natural right of suffrage, is a proposition that there is a natural right in one man to govern others, subject, it should be added, to a natural liability to be governed by others. Advocates for the natural right do not appear to be anxious to sustain the *liability*.

It makes no difference that the right is exercised along with others who have similar rights of suffrage. It is claimed as a natural, personal, individual right. But this exercise of the right with others, is certainly not a natural right. A community does not exist by nature. It is formed by association.

I do not know who is entitled to the paternity or maternity of the proposition that suffrage is a natural right, but the assertion of such a natural right argues either an ignorance of the nature of suffrage, or a disposition to use the proposition to serve the purposes of party, or of selfishness; and in either case it may well be presumed to have had its origin in Congress, — unless it be supposed that it is the offspring of some of the political lady stump speakers, who are clamoring for their natural right to govern others, before they have learned the way to govern themselves.

I do no injustice to any one. If there are few who express the proposition in these precise terms, there are many, some in Congress, and some out of that body, who have been clamoring for universal suffrage; and the propriety of universal suffrage can be based only on such a natural right.

But there is, and can be, no such thing as universal suffrage.

Those who clamor for it do not mean what they say.

Universal suffrage should be at least a right of suffrage in every one who could carry a ballot. In fact the child who is old enough to know and remember its own name is better qualified, in some respects, to exercise that right, than many of those upon whom Congress has assumed to confer it.

But every one, — even those who sustain universal suffrage, — will admit that there must be some limit. What, then, is the limit of that, which it is said, ought to be universal? Twenty-one years of age, even among negroes, seems to be admitted. What else?

The rules, before the adoption of the Constitution of the United States, were different in the several States.

In some a freehold estate was required for its exercise.

In some a large, in others a small, property qualification.

The original rules in the different States continued for a long period. Changes came by an extension of the suffrage; in new States by way of bidding for settlers, — and in the old by way of bidding for votes.

These extensions have carried the suffrage beyond the line of a safe policy.

Persons unacquainted with our institutions, unqualified to participate in the government, come into the possession of political power almost immediately after their arrival in the country.

More recently greater extensions have been proposed, and some of them adopted.

The principal of these are female suffrage, and negro suffrage.

Female suffrage, the exclusion of which has been almost universal in all ages throughout the world, is in its present day and generation the offspring of a few masculine females, in conjunction with a small number of feminine males; and by the careful nursing of peripatetic petticoat demagogues, and the dandling of hermaphrodite aspirants for Congress and the State legislatures, has become a child of large proportions, claiming *rights*, and prepared to take an active part in the race of political contests for supremacy.

If it is not yet a power in the state, it claims to be a powerful agitation.

If there were a natural right of suffrage, I am not sure that the claim of female suffrage could be denied, for there is certainly physical power sufficient to deposit the ballot, and surely I shall not be so ungallant as to contend that there is not, on the part of the women of the country, sufficient intelligence to enable them to vote as wisely, and discreetly, as their masculine compeers. I have no doubt that there are thousands and thousands of instances where the wives would vote more intelligently and conscientiously than their husbands do, at the present day.

But as I do not believe that suffrage is a natural right, I may be allowed to make a suggestion or two on this subject.

God does not appear to have designed women for voters. Biblical history furnishes us no precedents of that character. When Abraham sent Hagar into the wilderness, with a loaf of bread and a bottle of water, it was not in consequence of any vote which had been taken in the household on the subject. He was submissive to the despotism which ruled his action in that matter.

The Queen of Sheba came to prove Solomon with hard questions. We do not read that she propounded any respecting female suffrage, or that any suffrage of that or any other character existed in her dominions.

Ancient history seems to present female political power wherever it appears, as despotic in its character, and I am free to confess, that if we must have a despotism, I very much prefer one of this character, rather than a congressional despotism.

Artemisia and Zenobia, however otherwise distinguished, do not appear to have made any stump speeches in favor of the ballot.

Christianity, which has heretofore been supposed to have assigned to woman her proper sphere in creation, made no provision for any right of suffrage. But those persons who a few years since desired an anti-slavery Bible, and an anti-slavery God, may perhaps wish still farther to improve Christianity by other Bibles and other Gods, and among the new revelations of this description we may yet have a dispensation which shall include the right of females to a participation in the ballot box.

If there was any natural right of suffrage appertaining to womanhood, we certainly should expect to find it when the new commonwealths were founded on the shores of Massachusetts.

But there is no evidence that any such right of suffrage was exercised on board the Mayflower. The names of the heroic women who accompanied their husbands to the hardships of the wilderness, and who perished in the inclemency of the winter at Plymouth, are not found subscribed to the celebrated compact which gave a republican government to that colony.

We read in the eloquent words of a distinguished son of New Hampshire, of " chilled and shivering childhood, houseless but for a mother's arms, couchless but for a mother's breast ; " but there was no balloting there, nor any female suffrage in the subsequent history of the Pilgrims.

The beautiful Priscilla Mullins, who so naïvely inquired of that personable gentleman, Mr. John Alden, why he did not speak for himself, instead of playing the suitor in behalf of the valiant, but not good looking man of war, Miles Standish, — never carried a ballot in all the popular elections of the Colony.

If we turn to the Puritan Massachusetts Colony for evidence of natural right, we meet with no better success.

The Lady Arabella Johnson, almost worshipped among the emigrants, neither exercised nor claimed any right of suffrage.

If it finds no place in ancient history; if it finds no support in Christian teaching; if it was unknown to the early settlers of New England; if, in fact, it is substantially but the modern offspring of the enterprising female of the present generation, it is clear it cannot be maintained as a natural right.

Considered as a question of expediency, and not of natural right, there are some grave objections to this extension of suffrage, which have not been fully considered.

Theoretically, at least, all candidates for office should stand upon a reasonable equality.

The first effect of admitting female suffrage might well be expected to be, the removal of all candidates of the masculine gender over the age of, say, about forty years, more or less, from the pale of the candidacy. Young America has already done this to a large extent, and it seems is to do more, through and in favor of those who in four years lived a longer and deeper life than other persons. Female suffrage would finish the work, and set the seal of proscription upon most semi-centenarians.

Even ladies of a mature age love to look upon the face of a comely, personable young man, and of course such must find favor *prima facie* in the political canvass.

Gentlemen of riper years may have the support of a few friends who have known them in their youth, or are connected with them by ties of consanguinity, or personal friendship. But wrinkled faces, and gray hairs, cannot be expected to awaken any intense enthusiasm in the great body of female voters.

Let not the young man, however, rejoice in his youth, until he has considered whether his features have the requisite symmetry, and if not, whether he can present as qualifications for office a splendid pair of — whiskers, or an exquisite — moustache.

Even then there must be perils to be encountered. The canvass must be delightful, the visitings and solicitations for votes, — only there may be several Richmonds in the field, and consequent difficulties and uncertainties respecting the final result. But the contemplation of the ultimate possible consequence is awful.

You know that actions for breaches of promise to marry may

be sustained by circumstantial evidence. Fancy a successful candidate with a round half dozen of such actions on his back, when he has performed the express promise which he made in order to secure not only the vote of the promisee, but the influence which it was understood she could exert among an extensive connection. This is bad enough. Just imagine half a dozen *unsuccessful* candidates in the same forlorn predicament, exposed to all the dangers of circumstantial evidence, the success of one action being no bar to the others.

But I am forgetting that the primary causes will reduce the candidates to two, unless some one relies upon his qualifications, or his friends, to support him against the caucus, and runs as an independent candidate. An independent candidate! with a female constituency! The thing is absurd. His will be the most dangerous candidacy of all.

The caucus, however, presents preliminary dangers of a similar character, and perhaps of as great magnitude. The women who enjoy the right of suffrage must make that right effectual in their hands. They must attend the caucus. If they have the ballot merely to vote for candidates selected by what is sometimes called the "opposite sex" (no longer so, however, if of our party), it would be but as a mirage in the desert to a thirsty traveller. Of course there is a similar influence to be exerted, on a smaller theatre to be sure, in order to get the nomination of the caucus, or to secure an election as a delegate to the convention which makes the nomination.

But the struggle for office is not to be all on one side of the house.

The female stump agitators who are so clamorous for the right to vote, have no intention to stop there. Their desire is quite as strong, even stronger, I think, to be voted for, than to vote for others. Of course. Why not? We have, then, women at the primary caucus, to nominate for the officers who are to be elected by the political division which the caucus represents, — and to select the delegates to the various conventions, senatorial, gubernatorial, and congressional. Ordinary fair dealing will require that there be an equal representation. Nothing less than that ought to be satisfactory. Ordinary gallantry will yield something more. The masculine portion of the nominating conventions cannot be so unmindful of the power of the fair half of the community as to refuse to concede at least a full half of the nominations to the candidates of the fair delegates. We should certainly *expect* much more, as there comes in here the rivalry of the two political parties, each bidding for the support of this great power in the state.

And then we have next the canvass by the lady candidates, and their friends. There may not be so many elaborate stump speeches by the candidates which would be an advantage, — but other influences may be brought to bear upon the constituency.

The Duchess of Devonshire (in the reign of George III.) was a very beautiful woman, and a politician withal. She had not the right of suffrage, but she could influence those who had, and so she personally canvassed the borough in favor of Mr. Fox. Applying to a butcher (the story says), he answered that he would vote for her candidate if she would let him kiss her. She secured the vote!

If womanhood suffrage is admitted as a power of government, manhood suffrage and womanhood suffrage may not in all cases stand side by side in the contests for political supremacy. It is not likely that the one will be arrayed *en masse* against the other, for reasons "too numerous to mention," but the instances will not be rare, in which a man's political foes will be those of his own, or of his wife's household, as the case may be. If women are to be invested with the right of suffrage, it is that they may exercise it, and if they vote, they will canvass the district, man fashion and woman fashion also.

If they vote they will certainly become partisans, zealous partisans, as it is their nature to be, in whatever cause their sympathies are enlisted. Those persons, if any such there be, who expect that women, with the ballot in their hands, will purify the atmosphere of the hustings, and cast the oil of concord on the angry waves of party contention and political strife, may well take a fresh observation, and correct their political reckoning. Women who are disposed to cast their votes for honest candidates who will fill the offices with integrity, will soon be denounced by flippant stump orators of their own sex, as copperheads, cobras, or some other venomous kind of serpents, and will retire from the field of partisan politics, — where neither their influence nor their votes can be of any benefit to the state, — disgusted with the tricks and corruptions by which they find themselves surrounded, as many men have done and will continue to do.

All the reports which have reached us at the North represent the women of the South, exceptions of course, as among the most ultra of the secessionists, and of the advocates for the prosecution of the war to the bitter end; and, so far as the newspaper reports may be relied on, the female haranguers who stumped the Northern States, during the war, and who still ply their vocation in the service of a political party, were not a whit behind the chiefest of their Southern sisters in their denunciations; pouring the seven vials of their wrath not only upon the heads of the Southern white people, but upon all those at the North who failed to come up to their party standard. The way some of them "pitched into" (I think the phrase is appropriate in this connection) everything in the shape of constitutional law, so far as that law interposed any obstacle to their wishes, was a caution to constitutional law to keep clear of their path.

It is idle to expect that they will falter in the political "race of diligence" set before them, when they hold the ballot.

In times of strong party excitement men almost *in extremis* are carried to the polls to deposit their ballots. Why not women? Aspirants for office are always jubilant over the creation of a new one. Doctors are not exempt from ambition, and female suffrage may lead to — medical appointments in the interests of the party.

The inquiry may naturally suggest itself, whether, under such a dispensation, there is any extra danger that the officer elected may be, for a time, unable to discharge the duties of the office.

The duties of senators in Congress extend through a period of six years. Those of representatives in Congress, and in some of the State legislatures, for the term of two years. We always take the risk of disability by fever, and gout, and congestion, and all the kindred ills "which flesh is heir to." There is no insurance against such things. Here *may* be an additional disability. Well! — we must take the risk of that also.

The right and privilege of governing the country carries with it the duty of defending it by force of arms if necessary. In fact, this duty is generally considered as extending to males who have the protection of the government, even without a participation in its administration. If, therefore, women are admitted to the right of suffrage, and have all the rights of the men, why shall there not be a corresponding duty to carry arms and fight? There have been Amazons. Few, I think, since the invention of gunpowder.

But here is a new dispensation. When war comes, there will be questions of uniform, arms, equipments, and organization. Shall the usual habiliments of the sex be discarded, and the women train and fight, as they vote, "promiscuous"? Some objections are obvious. The morality of the camp would hardly be promoted by such an organization. Shall they form a separate corps, retain the female costume, and march into battle with all its impediments? The enemy can hardly be expected to respect the sex, marshalled in hostile array, and when the shot whistle, and the shells burst, the petticoats may be expected to fly, in more ways than one.

After all, the danger to the republic from the extension of suffrage does not lie in this direction. The disgust of the great body of masculine office seekers, at the prospect of yielding one half of their claims for office and plunder, coming in aid of common sense, is likely to constitute an effectual bar against a measure which might initiate such a state of things. With all the declamation about universal suffrage, and impartial suffrage, — with all the vehement advocacy of negro suffrage, because that may be made available to accomplish selfish purposes, — womanhood suffrage finds but a very limited support in the halls of Congress. Perhaps some of the leaders have found that in the nature of things there is no majority of two thirds to pass any measure over a petticoat veto, and are therefore more inclined to suppress even the primary power of a feminine will in household matters, than to clothe a refractory consort with a right of suffrage which might be personally antagonistic.

Over and above all, the great body of sensible women do not desire so far to depart from the political and social position which Christianity has assigned to them, as to mingle in the strife and turmoil of partisan politics.

But Congress has assumed to confer the right to vote for members of conventions to form constitutions upon the negroes of the Southern States, — upon persons who do not know what a constitution or a convention is, — upon persons who are ignorant of the nature of the election, — upon persons who do not know a month afterwards what the names were which they registered, under somebody's superintendence and guardianship, in order to secure a right to vote.

It is very easy to throw over all this the veil of a flimsy pretence that it is but a measure of justice to them, — that it is the only way in which they can be protected against the oppression of their old masters, — that they are entitled to it because some of their race fought the battles of the Union, and performed good service.

Undoubtedly some of them, picked up in various parts of the country, stood where the bone and muscle of the radicalism of Massachusetts ought to have stood, if it had had any bone and muscle for such a purpose. So persons imported from Germany stood as Massachusetts soldiers in the battles of the Wilderness, and were shot down by scores before they knew enough of English to understand the orders of their commanders, or even knew why they were there. Shall the freedom of Massachusetts be sent to the people of Germany for that reason? I speak thus unceremoniously of the radicalism of Massachusetts because it has been foremost in breaking down the safeguards of constitutional law, not with the bold utterance of Thaddeus Stevens that he would not stultify himself by pretending that the measures he supported were constitutional, — but generally under the hollow pretence that the Constitution authorized all the unconstitutional measures.

The earliest threat of disunion was an utterance from Massachusetts. The only successful nullification of the Constitution and laws of the United States came from Massachusetts, in her "personal liberty laws." The unconstitutional theory, by which the war powers of the Constitution trampled civil rights in the dust, had a Massachusetts origin. The notion of State suicide, was a Massachusetts "*felo de se*." The disregard of constitutional history in the allegation that the colonies became an entire nation on the declaration of independence, and that this entire nation formed the Constitution of the United States, leading to a mischievous enlargement of the power of the General Government, if it did not originate in Massachusetts, has had zealous advocates within her limits. And all the unconstitutional measures respecting reconstruction have found an unfaltering support within her borders. If all these unconstitutional measures and theories have not been the acts of the State of Massachusetts, she has given an unwavering adherence to the persons who promulgate and sustain them.

Let Massachusetts stand up and face her history, and not attempt to shirk its responsibilities by pretending that these unconstitutional measures and theories are founded in sound principles of constitutional law.

Has there been any fair trial whether the white people of the South would mete out as full a measure of justice to the negroes, under their new condition as freedmen, as they are likely to attain under the acts of congressional reconstruction? No, no; it is neither justice, nor gratitude, which is at the bottom of all this.

The white vote being so restricted, under pretence of participation in the rebellion, as to give the negro vote a preponderance suited to the purpose, it is expected that the conventions, managed by a few white men who are devoted to the party and desirous of securing the offices, will so construct the State constitutions that the States will be properly reconstructed to sustain the views of the radical managers, and secure them the support of the Southern States.

This is the natural exercise of the natural right of suffrage, pertaining to the negro. This is the manhood suffrage clamored for, — which makes the negro a tool of designing demagogues, and expects to overcome the will of the people who have understanding enough to exercise primary political power, by a pretence of equality as hollow as it is mischievous. I make no opposition to negro suffrage because it is negro suffrage. I have shared the right with the negro all my life without objection. But immense numbers of the emancipated slaves are too ignorant to comprehend the nature and character of suffrage.

Looking at the matter superficially it might seem somewhat strange that there has as yet been no effort to give the right of suffrage to the young men who are between eighteen and twenty-one years of age. Many of them served with great credit to themselves and great benefit to the country during the war. They have infinitely more intelligence than tens and hundreds of thousands of those who it is contended have a just right to it, and upon whom Congress has attempted to confer it.

The age of twenty-one, at which the minor attains his majority, is an arbitrary period, coming to us, as a limit from what, in the broad sunshine of our deeper life, we designate as the Dark Ages. Why not denounce the rule as a relic of barbarism, — remove the period of nonage to eighteen, or even sixteen, and thus give to the world another emancipation, and that of a more intelligent population, better qualified to exercise this right of suffrage? The deeper life of the young men who between the ages of sixteen and twenty-one fought the battles of the Union, and which so preëminently qualified them to direct the destinies of the nation, would seem to demand it.

But no, the negro of the South is the chosen vessel designed by nature for, and invested by Congress with, the primary power of government. In addition to the right to make constitutions in the States, — the general right of suffrage has been bestowed upon the negroes of the District of Columbia; and this is perhaps within the province of Congress under its general power of legislation over the District. Far be it from me to say that they will not vote as wisely and as honestly as many white persons who vote (not for men, but for measures) within the same District.

Undue extension of the right of suffrage tends to lessen its value and to make its exercise a matter of bargain and sale. Evils of this description have increased within the last few years, and are of perilous magnitude at the present time.

When we shall have attained to the conviction that suffrage is a right derived from Association, and that it is the primary power of a republic to be exercised for the purposes of establishing and maintaining good government, — and therefore rightfully to be exercised by persons qualified for its exercise, whether negroes or white persons, and none others, — we shall have learned the first principle which lies at the foundation of a republican government. If we can then make a practical application of the principle we shall have done much to secure the perpetuity of our institutions.

But how is it possible that a majority of those who now by constitutional provisions or statutes possess this right are to be persuaded of the truth of the principle, and that their own interest requires reform, while there are so many demagogues whose interest it is to mislead them? And until such a conviction reaches a majority of the voters how is the reformation to have a commencement?

Even if the principle were accepted as true, there are difficulties attending its application, inasmuch as there is no practical standard by which a precise and definite admeasurement of qualifications can be made in each particular case. But there may be an approach to it. Property qualifications are unsatisfactory, and yet the acquisition of property furnishes some evidence of intelligence, and the possession of property gives an additional interest in the maintenance of government, the protection of property as well as of persons being among the duties of government.

Massachusetts is entitled to the credit of having done something in the right direction when she required as a qualification that a person should be able to read and write, but even this restriction has caused great dissatisfaction among the class who clamor for manhood suffrage.

I will dismiss this branch of the subject at the present time with an extract from the New York Times, a paper which has the difficult part to play, of attempting to maintain some adherence to principle, and at the same time to keep within the ranks of its party.

"Universal Suffrage South."

"Universal suffrage, — exercised with independence and intelligence, — may be regarded as an indispensable element and condition of republican government. But experience shows that it may also be made a most powerful and fatal weapon, in the hands of unscrupulous power, to crush out all real liberty and bolster up an arbitrary and irresponsible tyranny. The Emperor of France has founded his throne upon universal suffrage. There is no country in the world where the suffrage is so absolutely free and universal, as in France; and there is no government in the world more arbitrary than that which it has established. The reason is that the suffrage of the people of France, instead of being independent, is simply the tool which the central authority uses to accomplish its own purposes. The great mass of the French peasants are ignorant, utterly without experience in affairs of government, dazzled by traditions, credulous of promises, and responding promptly and subserviently to appeals, representations, and demands made upon them from imperial quarters.

"At the elections the agents and committees of the Emperor

issue their letters of advice, — their arguments sustaining their theories, — their glowing pictures of the condition of the country, and their still more glowing promises for the future, and scatter them lavishly throughout the Empire. The coarser instruments of pressure are not neglected. The military 'regulate' the elections and preserve order. The civil officials represent, perhaps somewhat urgently, the expectations and wishes of the government, — their own hopes of preferment depending largely on their success.

"And so it happens that universal suffrage in France, — being simply a tool in the hands of the central power, instead of an independent expression of the intelligent popular will, — has founded and sustains one of the most arbitrary and despotic governments in Europe.

"The negro vote in the Southern States is exactly adapted to the same kind of management. At the very lowest estimate it constitutes *one third* of the popular vote of the Southern States, and is thus, in skilful hands, a weapon of sufficient power to control them. The negroes now admitted to the suffrage are, as a body, utterly ignorant — unable to read the ballots they are empowered to cast, — wholly inexperienced in public affairs, — incapable of foresight and provident preparation even for their own future, and far more incapable of any regard whatever for the future of the State or the nation, — accustomed to obey orders they receive from others, and taught, by precept and experience, to regard with distrust and animosity the community in which they live. Naturally and almost inevitably they look to some outside source for their instructions: and of course they do not look in vain.

"An Executive Committee of the Radical Party in Congress has taken charge of this matter, and has virtually taken charge of the negro vote in the Southern States. It does precisely for that vote what the agents of the French Emperor do for the peasantry vote throughout France, and by very much the same appliances. It prints documents and scatters them through the South. It employs agents, lecturers, and missionaries of its own views among the negro voters. And through its alliance with the dominant authority in the government, it has quite as complete command of the military authority, which is now supreme in the Southern States, and of the agents and subordinates of the Freedman's Bureau, as the French Emperor has of the Prefets and other officials of the Empire.

"We find in the Rochester Express a somewhat detailed statement of the operations of this committee, which we copy in another column of the Times as a matter of general interest. It seems that during the eight months from April to December of the present year, this committee has collected from members and employees of Congress, and from other sources, the sum of $42,673, and has disbursed $39,153 — the most of which has been devoted to the employment of agents to organize, discipline, and instruct the negroes of the Southern States in voting. They have employed directly in this work one hundred and seventy-eight persons, besides aiding through local committees as many more. But the most effective agency in the prosecution of the work they have undertaken is that of the *Secret Loyal Leagues*, which under the direction of the central authority have extended their organized and secret operations into every section of the South, and have contributed more than anything else to the consolidation of the negro vote. This effort has already been attended with a very great degree of success. The committee count upon that vote as sufficient to secure, first, the nomination, and next the election, of a radical republican President."

The third danger, greater than all, — one which in fact creates in a great measure the other two, is, —

An undue desire for office, — a hankering after place and power, — not to serve one's country, but for the promotion of selfish purposes.

Whether this, with the corruption attending it, is the *immedicabile vulnus* of the republic, or whether a remedy may be found, is perhaps the great problem which remains for solution. If there is no medicine to cure, or at least to check, this raging ulcer, the days of the body politic are surely numbered.

An efficient restriction of the suffrage, if practicable, might accomplish something towards the prevention of the frauds attendant upon the constant struggle for office. If that may not be expected, how are we to escape from this danger?

If a reasonable system could be devised, so that the suffrage, while it should be the main instrument of the election, should not alone perfect it, that might tend to a reformation.

It may deserve consideration whether a combination of suffrage with somewhat of the element of chance would not present a fair prospect of a partial remedy. There would, in such a system, be less opportunity for the excitement of prejudice and passion, and less temptation to bribery, and other means of corruption.

It may be objected, that so far as it should make the selection of rulers dependent upon chance, it would be a departure from the principle of a popular government. But if the chance relates to the selection of the candidates, and not to the final determination of the election, the objection is in a great measure overcome. Even if it should be made the means of the final determination and perfection of the election, by a selection among candidates already designated by the suffrage, it will decrease the temptation to bribery and fraud, and perhaps be most effective for that purpose.

We must recollect that we are surrounded with difficulties, and reduced to a choice between such expedients as seem best calculated to effect the desired object.

But is *Chance*, as the final determinator of an election, so very objectionable ?

I have long been of opinion that the course of our colleges, in exciting the personal ambition of the students by the offer of rewards in the shape of "appointments" to be performed at Commencement, has a most mischievous tendency, exciting to personal rivalry and evil passions, and ending, with many, in grievous disappointment and discouragement ; and that if public exhibitions are expedient upon such occasions, there should be an opportunity for all to exhibit their talents and acquirements, — or if that is impracticable, then, that it were better that a selection should be made by lot, — which would save disappointment and its attendant evils. And I hope that the day will come when this will be found to be true, and adopted as the rule ; although it must be admitted that the signs of the times are not full of encouragement. I fear that the clergy are largely responsible for the failure of the experiment which has been made upon that subject.

But nervous disease and premature death, occasioned by this educational pressure upon the brain, — disease and death increasing at a fearful rate, particularly among females, — may at last awake ambitious parents to a realization of the danger, and cause an improvement in our educational institutions.

And I would fain hope, that the principle of chance may to some extent be incorporated into our popular elections, and the excitement attendant upon them be thereby allayed, — if no other method may be found effectual to stop this miserable scramble for office.

Mischievous ambition, however, does not always exhibit itself in a direct attempt to procure office. It appears at "Bay

State" and "Fraternity" lectures, seeking notoriety by the advocacy of new theories of social life, as well as of political government, and in efforts, in various ways, not to improve the world in which we live, but to create a new one; all of which tend more or less to the disturbance of good government and the peace of society. It occupies the pulpit with denunciations of every one who differs from the political views of the preacher. It manifests itself at literary festivals, pours forth its scorn upon conservatism, canonizes the negro, and confers upon radicalism its apotheosis. An oration upon a *literary subject* before a literary society is the exception, and not the rule. Literary topics do not command the cheers, not to say huzzas and shouts, which are liberally conferred upon that frothy political declamation, which partisan newspapers call eloquence.

Unhallowed personal ambition seizes upon everything that may possibly be brought in aid of its aspirations, and corrupts it. Upon the moral opinions of the community, — upon the sympathies of our nature. How many demagogues, within the last few years, have succeeded in placing themselves in office by a pretence of friendship for temperance, or of sympathy for the slave.

This ambition packs the primary caucus, — corrupts the nominating convention, — stuffs the sleeve of the presiding officer with ballots for the candidate of the clique, to be placed adroitly upon the table, — or slily slips enough of those for the opposing candidate under it, to secure the right nomination.

This it is that leads to nominations not fit to be made, — to the employment of hireling writers to manufacture material to order, suited to the elevation of the party, or the employer, — to the thousand and one lies, editorial or otherwise, which circulate regularly through unscrupulous partisan presses, particularly on the eve of an election, — to bribing of the electors, — to fraud in the returns, — to appointments of persons unqualified for the performance of the duties of their offices, — to the victory of party over patriotism, by and through which the leaders control the bodies, minds, and consciences of their followers (so far as they have any consciences), who, the most abject kind of slaves, are looking, beseeching, praying, for office; and as a result, to the reception of bribes by the members of Congress, and other legislative bodies, and to the passage of acts through which the interest of the individual is subserved, and the public treasury defrauded.

But the particular crowning mischief of this eager pursuit of political office is exhibited in the policy which has been pursued by the ambitious leaders of the dominant party, since the close of the war, for the purpose of securing to their party success in the next Presidential election, and to themselves the offices and emoluments, bribes and plunder which may be obtained as a consequence of that success.

The time has been when I should have spoken of *honor*, in connection with office derived from political success, but that time has gone by. The struggle for office, not with motives of patriotism, — not with the legitimate desire of serving the best interests of the country, — not for the promotion of the welfare of the people of the State, or of the human race ; but for the party ends of an engrossing selfishness, and lately with the express view of plundering the public, and those who have business with public affairs, has shorn political office of the honor which was once an attendant upon it ; and if, at the present day, the presumption is not, that a person holding a political office has obtained it by indirect means, it requires at least affirmative evidence of some kind, to show that the converse of that proposition is an assured truth.

The war was waged, on the part of the North, professedly for the preservation of the integrity of the Union, assailed by the rebellion ; and the profession was, in the outset, the reality. The success of the war was to insure that result.

The expenditure of hundreds of thousands of lives, and thousands of millions of money, in order to take vengeance on those who were in rebellion, however unjustifiable that rebellion might be, would have been, not merely the extreme of folly, — it would have been but the superlative of insanity.

On the close of the war the material interests of the country required peace.

The selfish interests of the partisans of the dominant party required office. And for the purpose of securing that great good they have kept the country in the turmoil of "reconstruction."

The President broke loose from the "great expectations"

which had been indulged respecting his fidelity to the republican party, so far as to lead to a suspicion that all the offices would not be distributed among that party. The denunciations which have followed could not well have been greater if he had committed all the crimes enumerated in the Decalogue, and added a score or two of others of lesser magnitude. Treason to the republican party! Treason to the nation would have been a venial offence compared to it. Appointments to office of any but from the ranks of the faithful! Congress fairly howled over the idea, and the echoes of the eager expectants sent the reverberations throughout the length and breadth of the United States, to say nothing of Europe and the island of St. Domingo.

When Demetrius the silversmith who made silver shrines for Diana, and the craftsmen and workmen of like occupation saw that their craft, by which they had their wealth, was in danger of being set at nought, they were filled with wrath, and cried out, "Great is Diana of the Ephesians;" and the whole city was filled with confusion, and rushed with one accord into the theatre, and all with one voice about the space of two hours cried out, "Great is Diana of the Ephesians."

But the uproar of Ephesus was but a feeble and subdued utterance to the cry which went up when the unscrupulous leaders of the dominant party discovered that their craft was in danger, by which they, and their brothers, and uncles, and nephews, and cousins three times removed, and other miscellaneous partisan supporters, had their wealth. They rushed with one accord into the halls of Congress, and into conventions, and fraternity lecture rooms, and mass meetings,—and sometimes even into the pulpits, and from that day to this, for the space of about two years, they have in these, and various other places, cried out, Great is the republican party, and great is its love for the negro, and great were the achievements of the negro soldiers, and great is negro suffrage, which may enable us, through an efficient military despotism, to carry the next Presidential election, and secure the offices, and powers, and salaries, and *other emoluments*, to be derived therefrom.

We are not told what Demetrius and the craftsmen of Ephesus did, when the town clerk put an end to the uproar, and dismissed the assembly.

But we had no town clerk, with sufficient authority to silence the uproar in our case, and to dismiss the assembly which contains so many of the craftsmen of our day, — and so we know, from their acts, that they determined to carry the next Presidential election, Constitution or no Constitution. There is no other reasonable way of accounting for the unconstitutional acts which they have passed.

I say this in no partisan spirit. I would not say it here, if the question at issue, for the last two years, had been merely which of two or more political parties should gain an ascendancy.

But I say it because, with the views which I entertain of constitutional law, and of the unhallowed course of reckless aspirants for office and power, it is my duty, here and now, to make one more attempt to preserve the Constitution from destruction,— one more protest against infractions of its provisions, which have of late become so frequent, and so gross, that there is no well assured certainty that republican freedom will survive the fourth quarter of the century.

The partisan press is ready to follow the party leaders, — and the political atmosphere is poisoned by the fulsome slaver of flattery with which it bepraises the unconstitutional acts of Congress, and the venom, and froth, and scum, which it has spewed out upon President Johnson whenever he has attempted to arrest those unconstitutional measures by the power of the veto, rendered, however, utterly powerless by unconstitutional contrivances for that purpose.

The President is deprived, by what purports to be a statute, passed by two thirds of both Houses of Congress, against his veto, of the power not only of selecting his cabinet, but of removing a cabinet minister whose acts of arbitrary power ought long since to have caused his dismissal.

Everything is made to bend, not to any will of the people duly expressed, in a constitutional manner, but to an *assumed* will of the people, which is neither more nor less than the will of the dominant party in Congress.

You may say that this is strong language for this place. I admit it. But if I make my assertion good, that Congress, for the last two years, has engrossed to itself executive and judicial powers, — that it governs now by a military despotism, which is the creation of the will of Congress, and which represents that will to be the will of the people, — that it governs to secure the offices, and not to promote the prosperity and freedom and happiness of the people, — that it has thus not only violated the Constitution, again and again, by the assumption of powers which it does not possess, but has destroyed political freedom, endangered our republican institutions, and smote the industrial interests of a large section of the country with paralysis, — then what I have said, or may say, here or elsewhere, in condemnation of its acts, and of the vituperation which in and out of its halls is so liberally bestowed upon all who refuse to fall down and worship the idol, is not, and cannot be strong enough.

I am no partisan of President Johnson, but I honor him with all my heart for his firmness in endeavoring to sustain and vindicate the organic law of the republic.

What has given rise to the unconstitutional acts which have been passed by Congress, notwithstanding the President's veto, within the last two years?

I need have no delicacy even here in speaking of those acts as unconstitutional. The leader of the dominant party, in the House of Representatives said he would not so far stultify himself as to pretend that they were constitutional. If the party accepts his leadership, in their passage, it may well be charged *prima facie*, at least by his admissions respecting their character.

But those admissions are in no way necessary to the proof of their unconstitutionality. That is open, gross, shameless, palpable.

They have not even the merit of consistency in their unconstitutionality. And the attempts to justify them are equally inconsistent.

The first and third of the acts, providing for "reconstruction" may suffice as specimens of this unconstitutional legislation, — this trampling by the Legislative department upon the Executive, and the Judicial, through the military power which it controls.

The act of March 2d, 1867, recites, —

That "no legal State governments or adequate protection for life or property now exist in the rebel States of Virginia," &c., and that "it is necessary that peace and good order should be enforced in said States until loyal and republican State governments can be legally established," and therefore enacts, "that said rebel States shall be divided into military districts, and made subject to the military authority of the United States;" "that it shall be the duty of the President to assign to the command of each of said districts an officer of the army not below the rank of brigadier-general, and to detail a sufficient military force to enable such officer to perform his duties, and enforce his authority within the district to which he is assigned;" "that it shall be the duty of each officer, assigned as aforesaid, to protect all persons in their rights of person and property, to suppress insurrection, disorder, and violence" [except of course his own violence, and that which he orders], "and to punish, or cause to be punished, all disturbers of the public peace, and criminals, and to this end he *may allow local civil tribunals to take jurisdiction of and to try offenders*, *or*, WHEN IN HIS JUDGMENT IT MAY BE NECESSARY FOR THE TRIAL OF OFFENDERS, HE SHALL HAVE POWER TO ORGANIZE MILITARY COMMISSIONS OR TRIBUNALS FOR THAT PURPOSE; AND ALL INTERFERENCE UNDER COLOR OF STATE AUTHORITY WITH THE EXERCISE OF MILITARY AUTHORITY UNDER THIS ACT SHALL BE NULL AND VOID."

The military commander who should desire more ample authority than this must be somewhat unreasonable.

But there are some restrictions upon it. The laws and regulations for the government of the army are not to be affected by the act except so far as they conflict with its provisions. How far is that? Persons arrested are to be tried without unnecessary delay, of which the district commander is of course to be the judge; no cruel or unusual punishment is to be inflicted, — that is, none deemed by military law and officers to be cruel or unusual, — whether bucking and tying up by the thumbs and other tortures are to be deemed cruel or unusual is not said; no sentence of a military tribunal affecting the life or liberty of any person is to be executed until it is approved by the officer in command of the district, and even with his approval, no person is to be murdered by military authority without the approval of the President.

The limitations are not very formidable, unless it be the last, which may perhaps be regarded as rather stringent.

It is next provided that when the people of any one of said States shall have formed a constitution of government in conformity with the Constitution of the United States in all respects, framed by a convention of delegates elected by the male citizens of said State twenty-one years old and upward, of whatever race, color, or previous condition, who have been resident in the State for one year previous to the day of election (thousands and thousands of whom do not know what a constitution means), with the exception of persons disfranchised; and when such constitution shall provide that the elective franchise shall be enjoyed by all such persons as have the qualifications for electors of delegates (idiots and all other persons *non compos mentis*, — and negroes too ignorant to know what or who they are voting for, included); and when such constitution shall be ratified by a majority of the persons voting, &c., and shall have been submitted to Congress for examination and approval, *and Congress shall have approved the same;* and when the State legislature shall have adopted the proposed 14th article of amendment to the Constitution of the United States (which it cannot do unless the State is a State in the Union), and when that article shall have become a part of the constitution, — then, all these things having happened, the State shall be declared entitled to representation in Congress, &c.

But until the people of said States shall be by law admitted to representation in Congress (the two houses having bargained with each other not to admit any representation without the consent of both), "any civil government which may exist therein shall be *deemed provisional only, and in all respects subject to the paramount authority of the United States*, at any time to abolish, modify, control, or supersede the same," &c.

Then came a supplemental act of March 23d, providing for the calling of conventions with ample provisions to secure the ascendancy of military authority; and after this a supplement to the supplement, July 19, 1867, declaring that it was the true intent and meaning of the act of March 2d, and of the supplementary act of March 23d, that "the governments then existing in the rebel States of Virginia," &c., "were not legal State governments; and that thereafter said governments, if continued, were to be continued subject in all respects to the military commanders of the respective districts, and to the paramount authority of Congress."[1]

[1] There seems, after all, to have been an omission in the Acts of Reconstruction, or

It was further enacted "that the commander of any district named in said act shall have power, subject to the disapproval of the general of the army of the United States, and to have effect till disapproved, whenever in the opinion of such commander the proper administration of said act shall require it, to suspend or remove from office, or from the performance of official duties, and the exercise of official powers, any officer or person holding, or exercising, or professing to hold or exercise, any civil or military office, or duty in such district, under any power, election, appointment, or authority derived from, or granted by, or claimed under, any so-called State, or the government thereof, or any municipal or other division thereof; and upon such suspension or removal, such commander, subject to the disapproval of the general as aforesaid, shall have power to provide, from time to time, for the performance of the said duties of such officer or person so suspended or removed, by the detail of some competent officer or soldier of the army, or by the appointment of some other person to perform the same, and to fill vacancies occasioned by death, resignation, or otherwise."

If Congress were to govern the territories, over which the United States has full power of legislation, with such unmitigated despotic military authority, it would be rank tyranny. How much better is it — nay, how much worse it is, — when States in the Union are subjected to it; whether to gratify the vindictive spirit, or to promote the selfish purposes, of the party leaders, is immaterial.

But this is not all, — I had almost said it is not the worst.

This unhallowed march to power proposes to strike down the Judicial department, as well as the Executive, and the States.

Another bill which has passed the House, requires the concurrence of two thirds of the Supreme Court in order to a decision that any law of Congress is unconstitutional.

"SECTION 2. And be it further enacted, that no cause pending before the Supreme Court of the United States, involving the action or effect of any law of the United States, shall be decided adversely to the validity of such law without the concurrence of two thirds of all the members of said court in the decision upon the several points in which said law or any part thereof may be deemed invalid; pro-

a military district commander has slept upon his post, or the Supreme Court has been guilty of treason against Congress. Texas, not having the fear of Congress before her eyes, has prosecuted a suit in the courts of the United States, which could only be maintained by a *State in the Union*, and she has been declared to be, and to have been, a State in the Union all the time, and the suit is sustained.

vided, however, that if any Circuit or District Court of the United States shall adjudge any act of Congress to be unconstitutional or invalid, the judgment, before any further proceedings shall be had upon it, shall be certified up to the Supreme Court of the United States and shall be considered therein, and if, upon the consideration thereof, two thirds of all the members of the Supreme Court shall not affirm said judgment below, the same shall be declared and held reversed."

There is no hope of the present majority in Congress. They are committed to their attempt to secure the offices to their party if their march is over the ruins of the other departments. The watchword of their radical leaders is, "No step backwards," and their army of office holders, and dependents, and tools, and expectants, reëcho it.

Some of the timid hesitate respecting this war measure against the Judicial department, but they have given in against their conscientious convictions heretofore, and may be expected to do it again. The arithmetic required to enumerate the newspapers of the party which will not swear to all their readers, that the acts of reconstruction are sound constitutional law, is very limited indeed. I think I may undertake to count them upon my fingers, — yes, confining myself to one hand.

The only chance of redemption for the country is, the *possibility* that the intelligent portions of the community who love their country, and have no ambition for its offices, — or none except that they may fill those offices for useful purposes and noble ends, — may shake off their lethargy, arise in their might, sweep from the statute book the unconstitutional enactments, discard with them the ruinous policy which has dictated them, and consign the conspirators against the Constitution to the obscurity which they deserve.

Let us labor and pray that the effort come not too late.

Gentlemen: I have expressed my opinions somewhat more freely than I should have done, were it not that I address you as members of the Law School, for the last time. My resignation of the office of Royall Professor of Law will be in the hands of the Corporation in the course of this day, and with this Address my connection with the School is terminated.

You are just entering on the active business of life. You will have, to a greater or less extent, influence, — places of trust and confidence, — if not political offices, — stations where you may do much for the dissemination of true principles of government, and of constitutional law.

Let it be my last will and testament, in this last official act, to bequeath to you, and to those who have gone before, and those who may come after you, the support of a republican government, and the preservation of the Constitution.

I take my leave with fervent wishes for the prosperity of the School, and the happiness of all who have been or shall hereafter be connected with it.

www.ingramcontent.com/pod-product-compliance
Lightning Source LLC
LaVergne TN
LVHW021429110826
845150LV00007B/2160

* 9 7 8 1 4 2 5 5 0 7 0 1 5 *